After the Cross

After the Cross

Hugh J. Schonfield

SAN DIEGO • NEW YORK
A. S. BARNES & COMPANY, INC.
IN LONDON:
THE TANTIVY PRESS

First Edition
Manufactured in the United States of America

For information write to:
A.S. Barnes & Company, Inc.
P.O. Box 3051
La Jolla, California 92038

The Tantivy Press
Magdalen House
136-148 Tooley Street
London, SE1 2TT, England

Library of Congress Cataloging in Publication Data

Schonfield, Hugh Joseph, 1901-
 After the cross.

 Bibliography: P.
 1.   Jesus Christ—Resurrection.   I. Title.
BT481.S38   232.9'7   80-27856
ISBN 0-498-02549-7

1 2 3 4 5 6 7 8 9   84 83 82 81

Contents

Preface

Christianity, as a religion in its own right, is in serious trouble. Its difficulty has arisen because of its fundamental belief in the deity of Jesus as God incarnate, which caused those responsible for the crucifixion—in the Church's view—to be denounced as deicides.

But now it is being increasingly recognized by eminent Christian theologians, notably in a recent book, *The Myth of God Incarnate*, that there is adequate evidence to establish that Jesus, a Jew, made no claim to be divine, and that the doctrine was a paganized interpretation of the early Church's conviction that he was the Messiah (Christ). The final step was taken with the definition of the Godhead as a Trinity, composed of God the Father, God the Son, and God the Holy Spirit, a step of a metaphysical character that transferred the native habitat of Jesus from the Holy Land to Heaven.

The reversal of the process that gave rise to the Christian credo has had to wait a long time because of the Church's power in affairs both spiritual and secular. Not until the Age of Reason could there develop a relative freedom to inquire into the validity of the Christian tenets; the urge to do so had as an incentive an objective interest in Jesus as a man. How much of what was written about him in the New Testament was true? Extremists went so far as to deny that he had any physical historical existence, claiming that everything relating to him was historicized myth. A literary analysis of the records, progressively assisted by archaeological research, could do much better, and, sifting the wheat from the chaff, could convey that behind the interpretations there was indeed a man, one essentially of his own time and nation.

To the conservative Christian these indications were none too pleasing, since they very clearly detracted from the representation of the Divine Christ, basic in the Christian religion. Consequently, great efforts have been made to introduce modifications and qualifications of the old formulas to preserve their flavor while tacitly denying their verity.

Many prominent scholars are now bold enough to state openly that Jesus was not, and did not claim to be, the Son of God in any supernatural sense. This is tantamount to a denial of the truth of the Christian faith, and among its fundamentals the doctrine of Christ's Resurrection and Ascension. It was the Resurrection, according to Paul (Romans 1:4), that effectively demonstrated that Jesus was the Son of God. For Paul, the truth of everything else he taught hinged on this event. Faith in the atoning death of Jesus was vain if Jesus remained dead, not risen and ascended to heaven (1 Corinthians 15:1–19).

Thus, for Christianity to have justification as a religion in this modern age, it must still hold on to the tenet of the Resurrection, even if it has to be diluted and qualified to an extent that is a virtual rejection of its validity. Defensive and apologetic attitudes are taken by theologians whenever the subject is expounded and discussed. Evasions and circumlocutions are commonplace, and an investigation that is wholly objective is well nigh impossible.

The most favored position taken is to limit acceptable testimony to the truth and nature of the Resurrection as reflected in Paul's first letter to the Corinthians, Chapter 15. There the very early claim is made that Jesus rose from the dead the third day after his burial, was seen by many eyewitnesses among his followers, and finally by Paul himself. These encounters with Jesus were apparitions or sightings and did not demand that Jesus was *physically* alive again, which Paul rejected. Yet Paul's risen Jesus is in a personal sense really alive: he is not a ghost. Significantly, no details are furnished of the circumstances affecting the Resurrection, such as, for instance, the discovery of the empty tomb by women of Jesus' company who went there on the third day, as reported by all the Gospels. Adherence to Paul, who had only secondhand knowledge, enables the modernist Christian theologian to treat most of the information given by the Evangelists as historically dubious and largely fictitious. What is tied in with the *physical* resurrection of Jesus, such as the empty tomb, is thankfully sacrificed.

Surely this is going much too far. We certainly need to be carefully analytical of the Gospel material, recognizing the variety of factors responsible for it—faulty recollection, controversy, Messianic interpretation, Christological evolution, borrowing from other non-Christian stories and legends, individual attitudes of the Evangelists, and a certain amount of invention. But even so, there remain significant pointers to the preservation of valuable items of evidence that put us on the track of what became of Jesus' body. *After the Cross* does not necessarily call for a miraculous answer, and our task is to explore all other alternatives.

The disappearance of a body is a familiar ingredient of detective stories; but in the case of Jesus, the issues are of major consequence, because of their effect on religious convictions. We must, therefore, guard against frivolity and antireligious bias. That is not difficult for the author, a man of faith who has attempted to get as close as possible to the truth. The first fruits of his research, published in his book *The Passover Plot*, were much more tentative than the results of a specific and full-length inquiry since undertaken and published here.

The reader will find in these pages a systematic analysis of the familiar sources as well as the employment of other pertinent material with which he may not be acquainted. It is hoped that the reader, regardless of whether he agrees with the author's conclusions, will be in a much better position to assess the worth of his own views. The case made in this book, however, cannot be erased by cold water. If it is to be set aside, more convincing evidence must be adduced in favor of any alternative.

For the most part, biblical quotations are from the Authorized (King James) Version. In a few instances, however, the author has made his own translations directly from the Greek New Testament, which are readily distinguishable by their modern style.

In addition to the biblical references, some early uncanonical Christian books are cited. These works are known, for the most part, only from quotations or in fragmentary form. In some instances, they are ancient translations of the original Greek or Hebrew texts. Because they were employed by sectarians, they were, therefore, frowned upon, and copies were destroyed by the orthodox. But they are an important source of early traditions, some of which could be reliable. For this inquiry, reference is made to the *Gospel of the Hebrews* and to the *Gospel of Peter*, both dating from the second century A.D. Of less worth, but useful, is the *Book of the Resurrection of Christ*, attributed to the Apostle Bartholomew, preserved in Egypt in the Coptic language. A collection of this material in an English translation is found in M. R. James' *The Apocryphal New Testament* (Oxford: The Clarendon Press, 1926).

1
The Riddle

This book is, if you will, a detective story. It deals with a mystery nearly two thousand years old, and conducts an investigation of clues and possibilities in seeking an explanation that will best account for the circumstances.

Briefly, it is on record that in ancient Judaea under the Roman governor Pontius Pilate a certain Jew from Galilee, Jesus by name, accused of treason and sedition, was executed by crucifixion at Jerusalem on the eve of the Jewish Sabbath at the season of the spring festival of Passover. His body—it being accepted by the Roman authorities that he succumbed to the punishment inflicted on him—was handed over before the commencement of the Sabbath at sunset to a highly placed Jewish well-wisher, who laid him in a new tomb close to the place of execution. The tomb evidently was above ground and was cut horizontally into a rock face, since it was closed by a large circular stone similar to a millstone. This flat stone, running in a prepared groove, came to rest in front of the opening, thus blocking access to the interior. Initially, this Jesus had been accepted by a small following as a religious teacher, and eventually as the expected ultimate king of the Jews—the Messiah or

Anointed One. Certain women of his following, who had witnessed where his body had been placed, visited the tomb early
on the Sunday morning following the Sabbath. They were star-
tled and alarmed to find the tomb open and the body gone.
What had happened?

This, the barest possible statement of the riddle, omits additional and divergent details in the documentary sources, which
will be examined later. It must be stated at once, however, that
the Christian Church, which reveres Jesus as divine, holds that
he rose or was raised by God from the dead, therefore preclud-
ing any need to seek an alternative explanation.

In traditional Christianity, the doctrine of the resurrection
and ascension of Jesus Christ is central and fundamental. The
Apostle Paul made this principle especially clear in his letters.
Certainly it is open to anyone to believe that a miracle, or series
of miracles, took place, and consequently that the Christian
creed is valid. Faith for many, even today, goes so far as to assert
that they have had personal, even visual, contact with a living
Christ. Therefore, they insist, it must be rejected outright that
any other interpretation of the circumstances could be valid, for
this would contradict the Word of God (as contained in the New
Testament documents).

Yet a considerable number of Christians are not so uncom-
promising. There are scholars and theologians who tacitly, and
sometimes outspokenly, cast doubts on the authenticity of the
Resurrection accounts. They acknowledge a strong mythological
element; but the clerics among them tend to argue in favor of
spiritual experiences enjoyed by some of the associates of Jesus,
which allow it to be concluded that death had no power over
him. In that context it is deemed permissible, although strictly
illegitimate, to retain the term Resurrection in relation to Jesus.

The issue before us, however, is not whether miracles occur
or whether the human personality survives death. Examining
the evidence, we are seeking to discover whether it points to
some clarification of the mystery that does not demand any
other-worldly assumptions. For this purpose we cannot attach a
superhuman veracity to any of the documents concerned. Nor
are we entitled to evade the fact that the proposition of resurrection carries with it very definite physical implications.

Unfortunately, we cannot approach the puzzle with complete detachment from religious controversy, because it was out of such controversy that certain ingredients of the reported circumstances came to be formulated. Moreover, in this matter, the truth of the Christian faith is at stake, which not only impedes an objective approach but creates an obstacle to the acceptance of any unwelcome conclusion. Most adverse treatments of the subject previously have had a polemical aim, which throws suspicion on any effort to treat it with judicious impartiality. Needless to say, no such effort can be expected from defenders of the Christian position; those Christians who have advocated a more rational interpretation have usually been scorned and repudiated by the orthodox.

Down through the centuries, probably no Christian proposition has been more hotly debated than the resurrection of Jesus, because of what it conveys. In the first Christian period, at least at the popular level, there was widespread conviction that eminent persons overcame death, were seen and spoken to after their demise by those who knew them, and that some of these individuals ascended to heaven where they became deities or demigods. Information about these occurrences (see Appendix) is furnished by contemporaries of the Gospel writers, so it cannot be concluded that experiences comparable to the resurrection and ascension of Jesus were not related about anyone else. It simply would not be true. Such tales were familiar both to the pagan and Jewish world, though largely unknown to the modern churchgoer. There was an accepted place for myth and legend in ancient times within the framework of religion. Though there are schools of western philosophy that would like to restore this link, the literalists effectively oppose all compromise. A proposition must be true *or* false; a circumstance must be fact *or* fiction.

This hard-and-fast rule is very unfair to what is told of the past, and indeed to much that is asserted of the present. We must be allowed to distinguish between different levels and qualities of report, as well as different intentions of what was objectively perceived. But the Christian fundamentalist will not have it so. Boldly he declares that what is recorded in the Bible happened as narrated. Therefore, the fundamentalist feels much more challenged by historical and mundane inquiry, yet insists that investigation must be conducted on a fundamentalist plane. The resurrection and ascension of Jesus, with all the concomitants of angelic appearances, were acts of God in *our* world. From that point of view, we cannot be held at fault if we take up the challenge at that level as objectively as is practicable.

We are to ask, then, was the resurrection of Jesus a reality, as claimed, and did he thereafter bodily ascend to heaven? Or was this resurrection story told by inference partly to satisfy Jesus' followers regarding what they believed about him and partly as the most welcome solution to the riddle of the empty tomb? How much of what is set down is invention, and how much may reasonably be relied upon as accurate?

These questions have been tackled by many writers, with varying motivations and also have inspired several novelists. A sizable number of these writers have much in common in what they conjecture may actually have transpired. The important thing about certain of these conjectures is that they are based on an analysis of the Christian records themselves and support what it was natural to believe: that the tomb in which Jesus was placed after he was taken from the cross was found empty because his body had been removed from it, whether by friend or foe. This was also the opinion of the women who had made the discovery, as the Evangelists testify.

Nevertheless, the Christian assertion that Jesus rose, or was raised, from the dead and ascended to heaven should not be dismissed casually (the two claims are inseparable). It is based on testimony ascribed to individuals who knew Jesus intimately, as well as to some who may not have seen him previously. According to what is related, Jesus was encountered physically alive after the discovery that the tomb in which his body was laid was empty. He was no ghost. His flesh and bones could be felt. The wounds inflicted on him on the cross were visible and tangible. He could and did eat solid food. Finally, as one version declares, Jesus was elevated to heaven in sight of his disciples, who followed his progress skywards until a cloud concealed him from view.

There is much here that seems realistic and convincing. But as shown in the Appendix of this book, comparable information is furnished about other noteworthy persons by writers of those days, and documentation substantially discounts the impression of veracity that the New Testament authors seek to convey.

However, we are not initially concerned with matters relating specifically to Jesus, but rather to the question of resurrection itself, especially in the messianic context. In the first century A.D. it certainly was believed by multitudes—both Jews and non-Jews—that dead people could be restored to life through the instrumentality of saints and sages. But a segment of the Jews further believed that in the End Time there would be a General Resurrection of the dead. Did they also believe that the Messiah would die and rise again?

It is important to raise this question, because it has to be considered whether the accounts of Jesus' appearances to various disciples after his death would have happened had he not been believed by them to be the Messiah. Here the nonappearances of Jesus, especially to his enemies, must be given due weight. The number of recorded "appearances" is very small, with elements of uncertainty in certain instances. No enlightenment is offered as to where Jesus was and how he was maintaining himself at other times, except for the singular statement in the Acts of the Apostles (1:3) that he was seen by his disciples over a period of forty days.

The earliest Christian document that argues emphatically for the resurrection of Jesus is the Apostle Paul's first letter to the Corinthians, written some twenty years after the crucifixion. Belief in his resurrection was by then already well established, since Paul quotes testimony he received to this effect. The testimony asserts that Jesus had risen from the dead on the third day after his execution, and lists those persons who had seen him, some of whom were still living. To this list Paul finally appends his own name, although, according to the conviction to which he subscribed, Jesus was by this time no longer on earth. Therefore, Paul had not encountered a physical Jesus who had returned from the dead.

Paul could fit himself into the list only by not giving any

information whatever that was evidential of an actual resurrection of Jesus. In all the instances he quotes, Paul could only speak of sightings or apparitions, which is not the same thing at all. This fact clearly weakened his claim to be an apostle of Jesus of equal standing with the official apostolic body.

Without doubt, Paul believed in the resurrection of Jesus and his ascent to heaven, but the belief had to be capable of interpretation in a nonmaterialistic sense. Many pagan authorities of the period would have agreed with him heartily. Yet there was no getting around the fact that one could not speak of resurrection where the raising up of a body was not involved. This was what made the resurrection teaching so dubious a proposition to many of the Corinthian converts. Paul's answer was that in resurrection the body is not replaced by spirit, but one body is succeeded by another, the natural body by the spiritual body of the same person. The first perishes but the second is indestructible. The body is sown in corruption and is raised in incorruption. Does Paul's argument mean that the physical body of Jesus perished as being corruptible in some kind of transformation which took place in the tomb? His attempted explanation of the resurrection process and of Christ's connection with it gets very involved.

It is obvious that Paul's interpretation, perhaps intentionally, rules out that Jesus physically rose from the dead; and what he suggests does not self-evidently create any distinction between the *post mortem* experience of Jesus and that of any other person. The same process is operative. It is only that in Paul's opinion it operated for the first time with Jesus, while with others it will do so at the Second Coming. Nothing is adduced in support of this hypothesis, and we do not have to entertain it as representative of what resurrection implied to the immediate followers of Jesus. In fact, Paul's thesis calls for the instantaneous transformation of the physical bodies of those believers still surviving when Christ returns from heaven, who accordingly would not undergo resurrection at all.

Flesh and blood, Paul claims, cannot inherit the Kingdom of God. This claim eliminates him as a witness to any physical resurrection of Jesus, since only if Jesus had returned from a state of death to resumed physical life would the term resurrection be appropriate. In all instances given by the Gospels of persons raised from the dead by Jesus, and no less in the case of the widow Dorcas raised from the dead by Peter (Acts 9:36–42), a return to normal existence is stated or implied. And, as already noted, Jesus gives physical proofs in the Gospels of his own resurrection.

The restoration of physical life obviously demands that where entombment of the dead has already taken place, there must be an opening of the sepulchre from outside; otherwise, the revived individuals could not emerge. In the account of the raising of Lazarus in John's Gospel, Jesus orders the removal of the stone sealing the entrance to the cave tomb. Only when this is done can he call on Lazarus to come forth (John 11:38 – 44). According to Matthew, at the death of Jesus on the cross, there was an earthquake that opened many tombs. This enabled "many bodies of the saints which slept" (i.e., were dead) to come out of their tombs and go into Jerusalem and appear to many people (Matthew 27:51–53). The bodies therefore must have been reintegrated. The Jewish rabbis claimed that no human body could be totally destroyed. Even if it was cremated, there would remain a minute bone called Luz, on the basis of which God would rebuild the entire frame and clothe it with flesh. Matthew asserts that, in the case of Jesus, an angel descended and rolled away the stone from the mouth of his tomb. If the stone had not been removed, Jesus as a physical being raised from the dead could not have come out. The power is not ascribed to him to break out by shifting the external stone from within the tomb. Neither does any source suggest that the tomb remained closed, or that Jesus reappeared by dematerializing himself inside and rematerializing outside, although John does say that Jesus could pass through a closed door.

To the immediate disciples of Jesus, it would be most unlikely that a belief in his resurrection would have arisen if his tomb had not been found open and empty, or had been found empty on being opened subsequently by some of their number. Since the disciples did come to believe and were changed from mourners to rejoicers, there is the strongest presumption that it is historical fact that women close to Jesus visited the tomb on the first Sunday morning following the crucifixion, and that they discovered it open and the body of Jesus no longer there.

The circumstances also gave rise to another immediately perceived possibility—that others, foes or friends, had already been to the tomb and removed the corpse to some other place. Could there be any truth in this conclusion, and what would have been the motivation? The issues have been argued by many, usually uncritically and unrealistically, for example by Frank Morison in his well-known book, *Who Moved the Stone?*

That a riddle exists is undeniable. Equally, there is no obvious answer to it. The traditions are contradictory and adorned with fantasy, and yet they appear to preserve elements of truth. To bring these out, the scope of our investigation has to be enlarged considerably. Ultimately, evidence that is not normally considered will put us on the right track and help us clear up the age-old mystery.

2
Faith in the Future

From the Christian point of view, faith in the nature of Jesus as the incarnate and immortal Son of God makes it impossible that he should remain dead even though he died on the cross, so far as his human body was concerned. "I am he that liveth, and was dead; and, behold, I am alive for evermore" (Revelation 1:18). As divine, the grave could not hold him. Consequently, it was expected that he would furnish convincing proof to his disciples that he was more than man, which they previously had not been sure about. Realization that death had no power over him provided the foundation for the new religion of Christianity. So it is represented in Christian teaching.

It is considered of little significance, therefore, that we have diverse versions of what transpired. Indeed, total agreement of the witnesses would be unnatural and highly suspicious. The strange happenings set down so circumstantially are held as proof enough that something remarkable and unexpected took place, of which the Christian conviction seems to be the sufficient and satisfying explanation.

It already has been pointed out, however, that the Gospel accounts represent only a *physical* reanimation of Jesus—not the manifestation of an undying god. This relates to the issue as to whether Jesus was the expected Messiah who would deliver Israel (Luke 1:68 – 75; 24:21). How could he be the Messiah if he had indeed perished without delivering his people from their enemies?

This issue was paramount for the original followers of Jesus, who were Jews. They could only propagate the belief that the crucified Jesus was truly the Messiah by asserting that God had raised him from the dead and elevated him temporarily to heaven until the day of wrath and judgment, which would precede the messianic reign on earth. This, indeed, they came to believe. Otherwise there would have been no Christian community.

Yet, despite some attempt to convey that Jesus had predicted his resurrection on the third day, as found in the Gospels, the original disciples evidently had not been anticipating anything of the kind. They were not aware of any biblical prophecy interpreted to mean that the Messiah would die and rise again. Testimonies to this effect were adduced later. The common belief, based on the Scriptures, was that the Messiah would abide forever (John 12:34), which is conveyed by Isaiah (9:7), and, as regards Jesus, was communicated to his mother Mary by the angel Gabriel (Luke 1:32–33).

Thus, the possibility of resurrection was not at first entertained as an explanation when it was discovered that the body of Jesus was gone from the tomb. It was held that human hands had removed the corpse for some reason or other. As much as Jesus had been credited as the Saviour by his devoted companions, it had to be admitted reluctantly that his death could only mean that he was not the Messiah after all.

Because the thesis of the Resurrection so dominates Christian theology, it has to be remembered that, in the time of Jesus, belief that the dead would be restored to life at the End Time was a comparatively recent addition to Jewish doctrine. It was endorsed by the Pharisees and Essenes with their exuberant eschatology, but rejected by the more literalist and rational Sadducees.

Prophetic messianism not only promised the restoration of Israel and the advent of an era of world peace and justice—the

Messianic Age—but the participation in this bliss of all the righteous of past ages. They would be raised from the dead to a new physical life on earth. But what of the wicked? It was suggested that they too might be revived for judgment.

In Isaiah we read: "Thy dead shall live, together with my dead body shall they arise. Awake and sing, ye that dwell in dust: for thy dew is as the dew of herbs, and the earth shall cast out the dead." (26:19). By the second century B.C., especially from the time of the great persecution of the Jews by King Antiochus Epiphanes, belief in the resurrection of the body was widely accepted (Daniel 12:1 − 4; 2 Maccabees 7:9 − 36, 14:46), and was incorporated in the synagogue liturgy (*Eighteen Benedictions*, 2).

What is clearly established is that resurrection, which is a restoration of physical life, relates only to human beings: it cannot apply to spirit immortals. Therefore, in relation to Jesus, his resurrection cannot be correctly affirmed in support of his deity or divinity. It would be relevant only if he was wholly human, and has its context in the Pharisee–Essene faith in the resurrection of the dead in the Age to Come. In that Age, all the righteous would banquet with the Patriarchs, Abraham, Isaac, and Jacob, who themselves would be alive again on earth. The Gospels make it clear that this view of resurrection was shared by Jesus.

The doctrine of Jesus' resurrection was of great value to the early Church, because it achieved several things. It witnessed that because Jesus was a man, it was now demonstrated that the faithful would indeed be raised from the dead as heirs of the Kingdom of God. The words of comfort to the poor and persecuted were to be taken literally and were not just figures of speech.

Then it showed that Jesus was truly the Messiah, because God had raised him from the dead as an act of priority. Searching the scriptures produced the evidence that the corpse of the Messiah would not be allowed to see corruption (Psalms 16:8 − 11), that he would be elevated to sit at God's right hand with his enemies as his footstool (Psalms 110:1) and that he would reign over earth forever on the throne of David (Psalms 132:11; Isaiah 9:7). One Evangelist even declared that, after his resurrection, Jesus had demonstrated from the scriptures that what had happened to him had been predicted, and had challenged: "Ought not the Messiah to have suffered these things, and to enter into his glory?" (Luke 24:25 – 27).

Thus, the testimony that Jesus had been raised from the dead was in every respect a vital one. As Paul put it:

> *If in this life only we have hope in the Messiah, we are of all men most miserable. But now is the Messiah risen from the dead, and become the firstfruits of them that slept. For since by man came death, by man also the resurrection of the dead. For as in Adam all die, even so in the Messiah shall all be made alive. But every man in his own order: Messiah the firstfruits; afterward they that are Messiah's at his coming (1 Corinthians 15:19–23).*

By the deification of Jesus and the transference of the abode of the righteous from earth to heaven, the orthodox position of Christianity ultimately deprived the resurrection doctrine of its major justification.

For purposes of this investigation, what comes out so strongly is that a conviction of Christ's resurrection first offered a restoring confidence in his messiahship, and second a guarantee that the promises made to Israel were truthful, especially to the righteous poor and oppressed. Once the proposition had been put forward as an alternative explanation of the empty tomb to the natural one—that the body had been removed by human hands—there would be an eager desire to believe it. Some would be more readily persuaded than others; but for those who grieved bitterly, yet hoped against hope, there was really no need for confirmatory visitations of angels or even appearances of the risen Jesus. The welcome solution to the puzzle commended itself.

It is unnecessary to discount totally that things actually happened that lent themselves to interpretation in a psychic or supernatural sense once the key to the mystery in terms of resurrection had been offered. In such an atmosphere of exuberant relief, there would be every inducement for imagination and autosuggestion to play its part. Later teaching needs would invest certain claims with a precise expression, and to these would be added individual touches for polemical, edifying, and dogmatic purposes, leaving us to wrestle with the resultant minglings of marvels and actualities.

What we may adduce at this stage is that the notion that Jesus might rise or be raised from the dead was unexpected by the apostles and had not been entertained by them previously. "As yet they knew not the scripture that he must rise again from the dead" (John 20:9). Consequently, we may rule out the hostile suggestion that the apostles themselves had removed Christ's body to claim he had been restored to life. We cannot eliminate, of course, that human hands were responsible for removing the body of Jesus from the tomb. That is another question, and a vital one, which we will have to examine in due course.

Here, by way of summary, there are basic matters we must affirm. Resurrection, being a phenomenon relating to the restoration of physical existence to a dead human being, can only be claimed if it is agreed that Jesus was and remained no more than man, one who had died and had been entombed. If such resurrection did occur, it would have involved a miracle.

Furthermore, there must be some doubt, despite statements Jesus is said to have made, whether he expected his own resurrection or indeed his own death, since, at the time, messianic expectations did not envisage that the Messiah would die and rise again. There was some belief that the Messiah would undergo sufferings and persecution before his vindication, which had happened with the righteous Joseph, son of Jacob, with many of the prophets, and with King David before he took the throne. But that was not the same thing.

We can see, however, the appeal of the proposition of Christ's resurrection for his dispirited and partly disillusioned followers. It both restored faith in him as the Messiah and certified that there would indeed be a resurrection of the saints who had died, who would enjoy the bliss and bountiful provisions of the Kingdom.

But on what grounds did the belief begin that Jesus had, in fact, been raised from the dead? We turn to the circumstances as presented in the Gospels.

3
The Empty Tomb

The beginning of the resurrection narratives in the Gospels is the account of the finding of the empty tomb by some of the women of Jesus' company. They had seen the tomb in which his body had been placed after he had been taken down from the cross on Friday evening. Now, after the Sabbath, they had gone to the sepulchre early on Sunday morning only to find it open and the body gone. The women went to the tomb to cleanse and anoint the corpse according to custom, a task that could not have been performed sooner because it would have violated the Sabbath rest. We are clearly in a Jewish environment.

Certain Christian theologians have attempted to discredit this story as not forming a part of the earliest tradition, not simply because of the associated marvels, but because of the physical element introduced by reference to an open tomb and a missing corpse. Such an explanation detracts from the purely spiritual interpretation these divines wish to give to the resurrection doctrine. As we have already pointed out, the resurrection of Jesus—if it did take place—is a formidable argument against his deity. Intelligent scholarship could not fail to perceive this fact. Emphasis consequently is laid on visions of Jesus as sufficient evidence of a Living Lord.

However, though the accounts given in the Gospels vary considerably, there is close agreement on the matter of the women going to the tomb and finding it empty. The story clearly emanates from the Jewish environment of primitive Christianity, and represents such a strong and coherent recollection that the Evangelists had to include it, even if they saw fit to embellish it.

The Gospels of the New Testament are documents of a biographical character written for missionary and didactic purposes subsequent to the destruction of Jerusalem by the Romans in 70 A.D. The latest possible date for the crucifixion of Jesus—and the one I accept—is 36 A.D. Mark was certainly the earliest of the four Gospel writers (*ca.* 75 – 80). Matthew came next (*ca.* 85 – 90), followed by Luke a few years later, and John in its present form perhaps appeared around 110. These conclusions are arrived at through the examination of much internal and external evidence—literary, linguistic, historical, and traditional. The total effect of this evidence is overwhelming, and can be set aside only by those whose religious convictions demand a much more positive authenticity for all the Gospel statements, or whose resources are too restricted and their capacity for judgment insufficiently objective.

In the interval of from forty to seventy-five years before the writing of the Gospels, there were great changes in the environment and expression of Christian convictions, for which full allowance must be made. None of the Gospels was written in Palestine. The country of Jesus had been ruthlessly devastated by the Roman forces, and most of those who had known him were dead or had fled. Reliable, fresh information was hard to come by, and the needs of the Church in a gentile world demanded a different interpretation of Christ's significance.

Having thus been warned of the difficulties and the danger of snap judgments, in addition to the effects of a mythologizing process on the Gospel compositions, we are by no means led to the result that very little in these records is factual. By using the right criteria, it is not so difficult as it might appear from what has been said to isolate what, in substance, is reliable. The Gospels in the New Testament were not the earliest literary accounts of Jesus, and to an appreciable extent they employed written sources of which no manuscripts have yet been recovered.

Oral tradition and individual memory also played some part in shaping the narratives we possess, but not nearly as much as had been imagined in the past. The earliest written sources, since they emanated from the Jewish followers of Jesus and were designed for Jews, initially would have been in Hebrew or Aramaic. We have allusions to at least two such compositions. We can trace part of the indebtedness to such sources in the canonical Gospels, through literary analysis, through the nature of the sentiments expressed, and through the reproduction of Semitic idioms and syntax. Allusions to places, manners, and customs also offer some guidance.

The conscientious scholar is concerned with such indications, and in general for literary and background evidence of all kinds. It is usually very unfair to suggest that, having propounded a theory, he will adduce only those references that lend it support. I have often wrongly been accused by hostile critics of quoting only what suits me, and of looking around for evidence after producing some far-fetched notion.

We fully recognize here that belief in the Resurrection of Jesus belongs to the oldest Christian teaching. But in the information furnished there well could be traces of circumstances that by no means assured that the prevailing explanation was the correct one. Certainly it was not the one that initially presented itself, or even the one that appeared probable to the disciples who had been so close to Jesus.

Let us now look at the four canonical versions of the discovery of the empty tomb. The earliest is Mark, which unfortunately is incomplete and breaks off abruptly due to a defective manuscript. The present ending of the Gospel is acknowledged to be a later addition, and there is an alternative version.

At sunrise on Sunday morning, according to this version, three women disciples of Jesus, led by Mary of Magdala, set out from Jerusalem carrying spices to anoint the body of Jesus in the sepulchre where it had been placed on Friday evening. As they approached the spot, they were confronted with the problem of how to remove the great stone which covered the entrance. To their surprise, however, the tomb was open, and they went in. They were frightened by a young man in a long white robe sitting on the right side. "Don't be afraid," he said. "You are looking for Jesus of Nazareth, who was crucified. He is risen. He is not here. There is the place where they laid him. Go now, and tell his disciples, and Peter, that he is going ahead of you back to Galilee. You will see him there, as he told you." (According to Mark 14:28, on the way to the Garden of Gethsemane after the Last Supper, Jesus had informed the apostles that when he had risen he would precede them to Galilee.) Trembling and amazed, the women fled from the sepulchre, and told no one of their experience, for they were afraid.

This account is very straightforward and comparatively matter-of-fact. No attempt is made to suggest that the young man encountered in the tomb was other than human. He could have been an Essene, since he was robed in a white garment. In addition, no explanation is offered of how he came to be there or why he was entrusted with the message he delivered. Did he know the women would visit the tomb, and was he there to await their arrival, or did he have some other purpose? As we shall learn, it was risky for a man to be found without good reason at a tomb where there had been interference with a burial.

The man (or was it an angel?) was ready with words that, if genuine, he could not have obtained from any earthly source except Jesus himself. The speech, however, when we examine it, is highly suspect. It may be attributed either to the author of the Gospel or to his source. If the author was Mark, the interpreter of Peter (according to the tradition referred to by Papias in the second century in his work on the *Dominical Oracles*), he could have been quoting Peter. This could explain the curious command, "Tell his disciples, *and* Peter." After all, Peter was one of the disciples. Why was there a requirement that he should be specially told? If Peter was the narrator, he might have chosen to stress his special relationship to Jesus, of which he was very proud. We note that Mark does bring Peter uniquely into conjunction with the saying of Jesus after the Last Supper, "After that I am risen, I will go before you into Galilee" (Mark 14:28 — 29).

This quote is copied by Matthew (26:32–33). The Galilean rendezvous is repeated in Mark by the young man at the tomb. Again this is echoed in Matthew, who, however, omits the words "and Peter," and in other ways seeks to revise and improve on Mark.

We are confronted here with something crucial. The young man's (or angel's) purpose is quite positively to inform the women not only that Jesus has risen from the dead, but that he has gone or is about to go to Galilee. Only when the disciples have returned there will they see him. This Galilean line of tradition completely negates the idea that Jesus appeared to any of his disciples while they were still at Jerusalem, as affirmed by Luke and John.

Unfortunately, the conclusion of Mark's Gospel is lost, so we do not know whether it contained some reference to the meeting of Jesus with his disciples in Galilee, as seems likely from Matthew. Neither do we know whether, in Mark's ending, the women remained silent about their experiences, or revealed at this time only that they had found the tomb open and the body of Jesus missing.

Matthew's version of what happened takes a more positive and dramatic line. The young man of Mark is clearly replaced by the angel of the Lord, who descends from heaven, rolls aside the entrance stone, and sits on it. While announcing to the women that Jesus is no longer in the tomb, that he has risen from the dead, the angel neglects to specify how long prior to their arrival this had taken place. The action has been speeded up for greater effect, and from what follows it is possible to infer that Jesus had barely left the tomb before the women reached it. This is further suggested by the account of the guards posted at the tomb by the chief priests, who became as dead men when the angel descended and rolled back the stone. Presumably, Jesus left the tomb while the guards were unconscious, while the women arrived just after he had made his exit, though evidently he was still in the vicinity. None of the canonical sources introduces any human eyewitness of the actual resurrection.

It is unacceptable to Matthew that the women were so scared at finding the tomb open, with a man inside who spoke to them, that they ran away and told no one. Yes, they would have been afraid, but no less full of joy at learning that Jesus had risen from the dead. Far from telling no one, they hurried to the disciples with the joyful news. While they were on the way they were met by Jesus himself, who confirmed the word of the angel. He was no ghost, for the women held him by the feet. Matthew does not give the reaction of the disciples to the message, but they did return to Galilee, presumably at the conclusion of the festival, and went to a mountain Jesus apparently had specified in advance (Hermon or Tabor?). It is stated that they saw Jesus there, "but some doubted."

Matthew supports the Galilean tradition of Mark insofar as Jesus does not appear to his disciples at all in Judea. When they leave Jerusalem to return north, the disciples still have no evidence that he is alive. But in Matthew the women do see him, and they are the first witnesses, as is Mary Magdalene in John's Gospel. Whatever testimony there may have been to this effect is ignored in Paul's account. The word of hysterical women would not have been considered very reliable by Paul. This is conveyed by Luke, who favors the Jerusalem tradition. In Luke, *two* angels appear to the women at the tomb and announce the resurrection, but they make no reference to a meeting in Galilee. The women then return to Jerusalem and inform the eleven apostles "and all the rest," but "their words seemed to them as idle tales, and they believed them not" (24:11).

John's Gospel makes direct reference only to Mary Magdalene going to the tomb early on Sunday morning and finding it open. She has no vision of angels at this time, although she does on a later visit (20:11 – 12), but comes running to Peter and the unnamed disciple of this Gospel with the report, "They have taken away the Lord out of the tomb, and we know not where they have laid him." The "we" suggests that other women had been with her.

Examining these varying accounts, it could well be a reliable fact that several women of Jesus' company went to the tomb early on Sunday morning and found it open and empty. It is possible, but not certain, that they saw a stranger there who spoke to them. When they came to believe that Jesus had risen from the dead, an announcement made to the women became appropriate. But we should not accept this description as factual. Against it is the evidence that it was not true that Jesus spoke of his resurrection to his disciples in advance, since they were not anticipating any such development. Furthermore, the record seems more reliable that what the women reported was that the body of Jesus was gone. Persons had been to the tomb previously and removed it. Indeed, if a message had been given that Jesus had risen from the dead, it would have been totally unnecessary to speak of any removal of his body. To the death of Jesus had been added a new distress, that the corpse of Jesus had been abstracted, and now how was it to be discovered what had become of it?

The thesis of the Resurrection thus becomes not primary but secondary. Priority has to be given to the probability that those who moved the stone also took away the body. The opening of the tomb was effected for this very purpose.

4
The Begetter?

Before we turn to alternatives to Christ's resurrection as the true explanation of the empty tomb, we have to be confident that we can eliminate this interpretation from the possibilities to be considered. We need to try to track down how the belief originated that he had risen from the dead.

Despite certain Gospel statements to the contrary, it is evident that Jesus had not given his followers any indication during his life that his resurrection was to be expected and that the fulfillment of prophecy required it. Thus, the disciples were not anticipating any such miracle. The empty tomb initially conveyed only that his body had been taken from its resting place.

Faith in the Resurrection was not readily embraced even when advocated, and the view survived that the disciples had gone back to Galilee after the Passover almost entirely unconvinced of such an occurrence. Jesus had decidedly not appeared to them alive while they were in Jerusalem. Had this not been true, reference to such a damaging tradition would have been totally suppressed.

Especially in the Lukan and Johannine records, we can see at work the shaping of a resurrection doctrine based on circumstantial accounts of various appearances of Jesus to his followers. These appearances derive mainly from the Jerusalem tradition, to be set down later in attractive cameos in a gentile environment. But none of the canonical Gospels claims that any human being had seen Jesus rise from the dead, or that he appeared to anyone *before* his resurrection had been announced.

The government of the new Jesus Party, known as the Nazoreans, was established in Jerusalem. The party line accordingly insisted on Jerusalem as the region of revelation. Luke largely reflects the "official" account, to which Paul also was indebted. So in the third Gospel we have a succession of incidents directed to conveying that Jesus had indeed risen from the dead, and had personally expounded the relevant scriptures to his disciples, showing that the Messiah must suffer and then be resurrected on the third day. Repentance and remission of sins was to be preached in his name among all nations *"beginning at Jerusalem"* (Luke 24:47). The disciples were to remain in the city of Jerusalem until they received power from on high (Luke 24:49, Acts 1:3 — 4). For forty days the visions and instructions continue; and then the time comes for Jesus to ascend to heaven. Not knowing this, the disciples ask him whether at this time he will carry out the Messiah's task of restoring the kingdom to Israel. Jesus replies that knowledge of the time is kept secret by God. When they were close to Bethany on the east of the Mount of Olives, Jesus blesses his followers and is visibly taken up to heaven. They follow him with their eyes until a cloud hides him from sight. They are still staring skywards when two men in white appear beside them to announce that Jesus will ere long return in the same manner as they have seen him go.

Here we can see plainly that the Resurrection is an integral and essential part of a new messianic mythology centering on Jesus. The deification development of the myth was called for later to meet gentile needs. We can see, too, as we have noted, that the basic myth required that Jesus physically had to be restored to life by a miracle. Luke stresses that when Jesus appeared in Jerusalem to the eleven apostles, they imagined that they were seeing a spirit. They were asked to look at his hands and feet, to handle him—"for a spirit hath not flesh and bones, as ye see me have." As further proof of his physical state, he asks for food and ate a portion of fish and of a honeycomb.

Without the empty tomb there would have been no resurrection myth. If the tomb had remained closed, it would have been believed by everyone, friends and foes, that behind the stone blocking the entrance the tortured body of the Galilean prophet and would-be king of the Jews lay at rest. But for a tomb found open and a body missing there had to be an explanation. The fact must speedily have become known to all the inhabitants of Jerusalem and to many thousands of Jews from abroad who were in Jerusalem for the Passover. According to the apocryphal *Gospel of Peter* and other sources, multitudes had visited the tomb on the Sabbath out of respect or curiosity.

If it had been claimed at first, and had been true, that Jesus had left the tomb on Saturday night fully restored to health and strength, he would have been present locally, and have been seen by others besides his disciples. It is not suggested that he was naked when he appeared to the women and later to the men. The wrappings in which he was buried were found lying in the tomb. Where had he obtained clothing?

The open and empty tomb, if this was reported to the authorities, would in any case have led to an inquiry and search for the missing corpse. If Jesus had risen, prudence would suggest that he effectively concealed himself or preferably got away from Jerusalem as quickly as possible. Recognition of this probability might be responsible for the Galilean tradition that Jesus had set off after his resurrection for Galilee in the north, leaving a message for his disciples that he would meet them there. It also should be noted that the man who placed Jesus in the tomb, Joseph of Arimathaea, mysteriously vanished (at least he does not appear again in the canonical accounts). Apocryphal sources appreciate that he would have been wanted for questioning.

A certain amount of vagueness and confusion in the records would not in itself invalidate the resurrection proposition. Instead, what we encounter is an endeavor to introduce a precision that would make the resurrection thesis more plausible and acceptable in places, where evidently the reports of Jesus' appearances were not definite enough to endorse it.

There is a curiosity about some of these recorded appearances, the suggestion being that only in private did Jesus reveal himself to his followers. At other times, those who claimed to have seen him, or on whose behalf it was claimed that he had been seen, had been unable to recognize him. Does this hint at an explanation of why he was not identified by other people familiar with his physical aspects? Certainly we find in the material we possess (Luke and John, the author of the present end of Mark, the uncanonical *Acts of John*, etc.) indications that Jesus could change his guise (compare Mark 16:12). Perhaps this idea originated and found a place in the records to account for and excuse the difficulty the disciples evidently had in crediting the Resurrection (Mark 16:11,13,14). Even when confronted presumably with Jesus in person "some doubted" (Matthew 28:17).

Among the precise elements we have referred to are the terms of the message delivered by the young man (or angel) to the women at the tomb. Here, the announcement of the resurrection of Jesus is very explicit, when certainly it could not have been. Information survived that the women ran to tell the apostles that unknown persons had removed his body, but not that Jesus had risen from the dead.

If, then, the young man's message, in whole or part, was a later invention, how did the notion of Jesus' resurrection originate? As we have pointed out, it cannot be the fact, as Mark intimates, that Jesus himself had told his disciples in advance to expect this event, since evidently they were not anticipating anything of the kind; and they did not readily respond to the idea that Jesus could have risen from the dead.

Consequently, we must then turn to what seems to have followed the women's discovery that the tomb was open and empty. They ran in dismay to tell the apostles, not of the Master's resurrection, but that human hands of persons unknown had removed his body from its resting place. This was unexpected and dire news, which needed to be checked immediately. "Then arose Peter, and ran unto the sepulchre; and stooping down, he beheld the linen clothes laid by themselves, and

departed, wondering in himself at that which was come to pass"
(Luke 24:12). A little later (verse 24) Luke conveys that Peter was
not alone when he went to the tomb.

A much more detailed version is given in an autobiographical
passage in John. Simon Peter is with the disciple "whom Jesus
loved" at the latter's house, when Mary Magdalene bursts in on
them with the report that the body had been removed. At once
the two men run to the sepulchre, but the other, presumably
younger disciple (i.e., John himself) reaches the tomb first. He
stoops down and looks in, sees the linen wrappings lying there,
but he does not enter the tomb. Peter approaches and goes
straight into the tomb. He not only sees the linen wrappings but
the towel folded up separately that had covered Jesus' face.
"Then went in also that other disciple ... and he saw, *and
believed*. For as yet they knew not the scripture that he must rise
again from the dead." They go back to the house (John 20:1–10).

The author of the memoirs underlying John's Gospel dis-
tinctly makes the claim that he was the first disciple to interpret
the evidence of the empty tomb and the neatly wrapped grave
clothes to mean that Jesus had risen from the dead. He conveys
that it was an inspired guess on his part. The claim is important,
and it could well be true. Who, then, was the man who made it?

The man who calls himself "the dear disciple" of Jesus bears
the name John in Christian tradition. He lived to a great age,
residing finally at Ephesus in Asia Minor, where, according to
tradition, he was induced to dictate his personal recollections.
It was believed by many that he would survive until Jesus
returned from heaven (John 21:20 – 23). According to Polycrates,
the bishop of Ephesus towards the end of the second century,
John not only had been a Jewish priest but of high priestly
status (*Letter to Victor, Bishop of Rome*, quoted by Eusebius,
Ecclesiastical History, Book V, Ch. 24). He claims to have been
known personally to the high priest Caiaphas (John 18:15). From
his writing he was evidently an educated man, and it would
seem a man of means also. He owned a large house at
Jerusalem, probably the scene of the Last Supper where this
disciple reclined in a place of honor on the bosom of Jesus, and
probably the house that became the meeting place of the disci-

ples after the crucifixion. From the Gospel, we are able to gather
that he had first been associated with John the Baptist, and
there are many reflections of the Dead Sea Scrolls in this work.
The sect of the scrolls (Essenes?) had strong links with the
Jewish priesthood.

An attempt recently was made by Dr. John Robinson to revive
the old identification of the "dear disciple" with the turbulent
Galilean fisherman John the son of Zebedee (*Redating the New
Testament*, Philadelphia: Westminster, 1976). But this relationship is out of the question. By tradition, our man is a priest and
is very close to the seats of power in Jerusalem. In his narrative,
he alone introduces Nicodemus, a Pharisee member of the
Sanhedrin, and can learn what went on in the council (John
7:45 – 53). He describes another member of the Sanhedrin, Joseph
of Arimathaea, as a secret disciple. He knows the personal name
of the high priest's servant whose ear Peter has severed at
Gethsemane, and also knows that it was a kinsman of that
servant who challenged Peter in the courtyard of the high
priest's palace (18:26). Peter had only been admitted because he
was in the company of this other disciple "who was known to
the high priest" and who spoke on his behalf to the woman
doorkeeper. John alone refers to Jesus as having been first taken
after arrest to the house of Annas, father-in-law of Caiaphas, the
reigning high priest (18:13), and he is interested in making the
observation that those who brought Jesus before the governor
Pontius Pilate would not enter the judgment hall because they
might incur defilement and be unable, therefore, to eat the
passover (18:28). When he and Peter run to the tomb, and John
arrives first, he only looks in; and though he sees the cast off
grave clothes, he will not enter, presumably because as a priest
he might incur defilement from contact with the dead. Peter has
no such problem and goes right in. John then follows once he is
sure that there is no dead body inside.

Here is a man, then, of Jerusalem, not one of the Twelve,
whom Jesus loved and therefore trusted, and who must have
loved him; a man of priestly stock, messianist and mystic, able to
exert a powerful influence on the humble, untutored, and
superstitious Simon Peter. Rivals in loyalty to the Master, it is

little wonder that Peter should be jealous of someone of such quality. Here was a man who could well have had the sudden inspiration to interpret what he saw at the tomb as pointing to the resurrection of Jesus rather than the removal of his body. It was a solution in accord with his faith and desire, and he had the learning and prestige to impress his startling conviction on his associates.

5
The Resurrection Gospel

The records indicate a great reluctance among the apostolic band to credit the resurrection of Jesus, as well as an inability by those who knew him intimately to recognize the "appearances" spontaneously as those of Jesus. Both these indications weigh heavily against the resurrection thesis as the true explanation of the empty tomb. It is, of course, narrated that Jesus did reveal himself on almost every occasion, but it may be deduced that the primary persuasion came from the conviction of the man we shall call John the Priest.

It was his inspiration, born of the strength of his devotion, that signaled that Jesus had burst through the gates of death, and who read in the signs at the tomb the joyful message that the Master had returned to life. It is significant that this revelation occurred to John when there had been no intimation of a resurrection from either man or angel, when no scripture had been interpreted as prefiguring it, and when there was no appearance of the risen Lord to John individually.

When we grasp John's significance, it throws a flood of new light on the Fourth Gospel itself. It comes before us uniquely as the Resurrection Gospel—the Gospel about the one who returns to life and is the giver of life.

In the closing chapters of the Gospel, after John's own belief has been stated, a first appearance of Jesus to another follower who loved him is described. After Peter and John leave the tomb, Mary Magdalene, who had followed them there, stays behind weeping. She sees Jesus, we are told, but does not know it is Jesus (20:14), and supposes the man to be the gardener. Jesus reveals himself, and so she becomes the first eyewitness.

The next story in John is of an appearance of Jesus to the disciples in a house where they are assembled. This time there is no doubt of who he is, for he exhibits the wounds inflicted on him. But one disciple, Thomas, is absent. So to reinforce that he is truly alive, Jesus appears a second time to his disciples eight days later when Thomas is present. So now we have the tale of the convinced doubter as an object lesson. "Thomas, because thou hast seen me, thou hast believed: blessed are they that have not seen, and have believed." The Gospel closes on this note. What has been set down is to inspire belief that Jesus is the Messiah, the Son of God, "so that those who believe may have life through his name" (20:31).

But the Gospel has an appended chapter describing a further appearance of Jesus to his disciples at the Sea of Galilee. This emphasizes the authority of the "Dear Disciple," whose own conviction of the Resurrection is really enough to overcome all doubts. He almost hypnotizes the disciples into believing that the man they encounter by the lake is, in fact, Jesus.

In the appended chapter, the disciples are on a fishing expedition, when in the dawn light they perceive a man standing on the shore. This, of course, is Jesus; but, we are told, "the disciples knew not that it was Jesus." No fish had been caught during the night; but now the man tells them where to cast their net to find fish. Immediately they are rewarded with a substantial catch, and thereupon the "Dear Disciple" declares to Peter that the man on the shore is the Master. The eagerly trusting Peter accepts this explanation and jumps into the sea to wade ashore. When the catch has been landed the disciples discover that the stranger is already cooking fish over a fire. He greets them, "Come and dine." Then we read the extraordinary words, "And none of the disciples durst ask him, Who art thou? knowing it was the Lord" (21:12).

Peter and the others could not have possibly mistaken the man had he been the real Jesus; they knew his face too well. Against the evidence of their own senses, they are induced by John to acknowledge the total stranger as Jesus. Strangely, and perhaps deliberately, no account has survived of the appearance of Jesus first to Peter, as alleged by Paul and Luke (1 Corinthians 15:5; Luke 24:34).

If the recorded appearances of Jesus were all of the same order—that is to say, if he presented himself in a variety of circumstances always as solid flesh and bone exhibiting the scars of his crucifixion, recognizably in voice and appearance the same familiar person as he was before—his resurrection might conceivably have to be entertained as one possibility in defiance of any natural explanation. But with the various accounts of a Jesus whose aspect alters, and who can appear and disappear at will, the assertion of his resurrection falls to the ground. It is credible that Jesus might have survived as a materializing spirit, which would account for the phenomena; but that, as we have made clear, is not *resurrection*.

We are left without consistent evidence in the same area as much antique mythology, where holy men and deities can exhibit themselves at will in any guise, and in the company of all those *post mortem* phenomena which psychical research seeks to investigate. But we cannot escape the possibility here of a pressure being built up by a devotee to induce more down-to-earth disciples to falsify the evidence of their own eyes as if by hypnotism.

John the Priest, passionately convinced that Jesus was the Messiah, the divinely sent king of Israel, presents himself as the pioneer of those who not seeing have believed. The Resurrection is his inspiration, shaping itself in the words of David, which came to be applied as prophetic, "Thou wilt not leave my soul in Sheol; neither wilt Thou suffer Thine holy one to see corruption" (Psalms 16:10).

Pursuing this clue through a careful reading of the Fourth Gospel, we see the mysterious disciple first among the followers of John the Baptist. After Jesus was baptized, this disciple and Andrew, Simon Peter's brother, go after him and later leave him, having become convinced that he is the Messiah (John 1:35 — 42).

From this point on, John the Priest builds up a portrayal of a miracle-Messiah who can perform wonders, not the least of these being the ability to rise from the dead.

The Fourth Gospel places very early the cleansing of the temple by Jesus, in contrast to the other Gospels. When the Jews on this occasion ask for a sign, he tells them, "Destroy this temple, and in three days I will raise it up." The author comments: "But he spoke of the temple of his body. When therefore he was risen from the dead, his disciples remembered that he had said this unto them; and they believed the scripture, and the word which Jesus has said" (John 2:21–22).

Continually the emphasis is on faith in Jesus as the passport to everlasting life. This singular Son of God "has life in himself" (5:26), so that he is imperishable and can call the dead from their graves. Jesus lays down his life, but only that he may resume it. "No man taketh it from me, but I lay it down of myself. I have power to lay it down, and I have power to take it again" (10:17–18). It is not God, therefore, who raises Jesus from the dead: he rises from the dead by his own power.

Shortly after this declaration, we are given the story of the raising of Lazarus, brother of Martha and Mary of Bethany, someone not mentioned by the other Evangelists. No other Gospel, therefore, relates this fantastic miracle, which seems designed to anticipate the resurrection of Jesus himself.

Jesus is many miles away when Lazarus dies, so there can be no question of a feigned death or the possibility of collusion. Jesus states specifically that Lazarus is dead when he refers to him as sleeping, and he returns to Bethany for the express purpose of reviving Lazarus only when decomposition of his body should have started. It should be observed that the tomb in which Lazarus is laid is similar to the one in which the body of Jesus was to be placed—a cave tomb with the entrance covered by a large stone—and that the miracle takes place on the fourth day, whereas Jesus rose on the third day.

When Jesus reaches Bethany, one of the sisters of Lazarus, Martha, runs to meet him. Jesus tells the grieving woman that her brother will rise again. Martha replies, "I know that he shall rise again in the resurrection at the last day." This enables Jesus to make the staggering assertion, "I am Resurrection and Life: he that believeth in me, though he were dead, yet shall he live: and whosoever liveth and believeth in me shall never die. Believest thou this?" Martha is not quite sure, and contents herself with affirming that she believes that he is the expected Messiah.

Jesus orders the removal of the stone from the tomb's mouth and calls loudly to Lazarus to come forth. "And he that was dead came forth, bound hand and foot with graveclothes: and his face was bound about with a napkin. Jesus saith unto them, Loose him, and let him go."

In this story, Jesus is demonstrating his power over life and death so that it can be no surprise or impossibility that he is able to raise himself from the dead.

According to John's Gospel, which alone records this miracle, the raising of Lazarus became known to multitudes at Jerusalem, as well as to the chief priests, who therefore wanted to kill Lazarus and Jesus (12:9–11). In these circumstances, it is being conveyed, there can be no reason why any follower of Jesus should be in doubt about his resurrection, since what Jesus had done for others he surely could do for himself.

The Doubting Thomas incident underlines the point that one should be able to believe in the Resurrection without personally having encountered the risen Messiah. John himself had believed in the Resurrection simply on the evidence of the empty tomb and the folded graveclothes and discarded napkin. A woman who had also loved Jesus perhaps needed more definite proof that he was alive again, since women were held to be so earthbound. So the distracted Mary Magdalene is made the first eyewitness. Despite the presence of angels in the tomb (20:12), when she does see Jesus, she imagines him to be the gardener of the plantation where the tomb is located. Not until he calls her by name does she know him to be the Master. Incidentally, and this may help tell us more about the Dear Disciple, the risen Jesus will not let Mary, a woman, touch him, though later he encourages Thomas to do so.

This Gospel insists upon the conviction that finally prevailed with the disciples: that for Jesus to be the Messiah who would reign over the resurrected dead, he himself could not remain dead. The disciples wanted to be convinced that he was indeed the Messiah and that their faith in him was justified. John the

Priest's persuasive contribution was the interpretation of the empty tomb as certifying that Jesus had brought himself back to life. To John personally, the interpretation had come as an inspired revelation, and he was positive it was the joyful truth.

6
Was It Theft?

The sources we have considered may conceivably, for those who believe that human beings do not really die, convey that Jesus on the death of his physical body entered the afterlife of the spirit world. For this no miracle was required, since it is held to happen automatically to everyone. There was nothing original or unique in Jesus' ability to make afterdeath appearances to those who had been his associates. Stories of apparitions in broad daylight, especially of noteworthy persons, were commonplace in antiquity and have been, indeed, in all periods.

But, as we have rightly insisted, such appearances are quite distinct from resurrection, which would apply to Jesus only if his physical body, the one laid in the tomb, was restored after his grievous wounds and sufferings to active functional life within some thirty-six hours of being conveyed to the sepulchre. The records, notably John, to a substantial extent seek to convey that this is what happened; but in doing so they have to assert that a stupendous and special miracle took place, which included the subsequent bodily ascent of Jesus to heaven. Factors we have investigated weigh strongly against the reality of the resurrection and we must therefore discard it as a hypothesis, and give our consideration to more naturalistic alternatives.

We must now concern ourselves with other conceivable explanations of the empty tomb, on the assumption that human hands were responsible for opening the tomb from outside (it could not be opened from inside) and removing the body. This, according to John, was what was first believed by the women when they visited the tomb early on Sunday morning and found it open.

Though the suggestion has found fractional credence, we may dismiss as too glib an explanation that the women went to the wrong tomb by mistake. When they encountered the young man at the tomb, he thought they might be followers of Jesus and tried to assist them. "You are looking for Jesus of Nazareth," he said. "He is not here." According to this suggestion, he then points out the real tomb, but the women are terrified and run away. The man could have been a gardener or custodian, it is said, and, on a cliff with many cave tombs, it would have been possible for the women to have forgotten from Friday evening which tomb it was (Rupert Furneaux, *The Empty Tomb*, New York: Panther Books, 1963).

On a matter of such importance, we may assume that the women would have taken pains, as Mark points out, to make sure they knew to which tomb Jesus had been taken so they could readily recognize it again.

One of the possible alternatives to the resurrection proposition is found exclusively in Matthew's Gospel. In a controversy that developed between Christians and Jews, it was apparently alleged, from the Jewish side, that if the tomb were empty it must have been because his disciples stole the body of Jesus at night to claim he had risen from the dead and thus deceive the people.

According to Justin Martyr, writing in the middle of the second century, the Jewish authorities in Judea had sent out emissaries to warn coreligionists throughout the world that:

> *A godless and lawless heresy had sprung up from one Jesus, a Galilean deceiver, whom we crucified, but his disciples stole him by night from the tomb, where he was laid when unfastened from the cross, and now deceive men by asserting that he has risen from the dead and ascended to heaven* (Dialogue with Trypho, 108).

In all probability, some such warning was sent out, particularly to counter the effects of Pauline propaganda in the synagogues of the Dispersion. But Justin is probably guessing about the terms of the communication, using Matthew as one of his authorities. We know that the Sanhedrin did send out apostles with letters to the Jewish communities abroad as a regular practice, especially on matters of religious concern (compare Acts 28:21).

If Jewish apologists were goaded into accusing the Christians of fraud, it was not unnatural. If the body of Jesus had disappeared from the tomb, as alleged, it seemed obvious that a human agency had to be responsible. And who, other than associates of Jesus, would have any interest in removing his corpse? They clearly stood to gain by the evidence of the empty sepulchre in proclaiming that Jesus as Messiah had been raised from the dead and taken to heaven. After all, it had been believed that Enoch and Elijah had been bodily taken to heaven, and there was a current teaching of the Assumption of Moses. If the body of Jesus could not be produced, a miracle on his behalf could be claimed plausibly.

Matthew seeks to rebut the Jewish allegation with a fantastic story, which could not fail to find a place in the other Gospels if there were any truth in it. Christian fraud has to be ruled out, Matthew conveys, because the stone covering the mouth of the tomb had been sealed the very next day following the crucifixion. What was more, the Jewish authorities had posted a guard at the tomb to keep watch until the end of the third day. This precaution had been taken because Jesus in his lifetime had declared, "After three days I will rise again" (Matthew 27:63). There was the risk that the disciples would attempt to help make good his words, and thus "the last error shall be worse than the first."

Matthew goes on to relate how this security measure proved of no avail, the disciples not being at all involved in what took place. At about dawn of the third day, the tomb was found empty by the women who came there. There had been a great earthquake, associated with the descent of the angel of the Lord, who had come and rolled back the stone from the door and sat upon it. "His countenance was like lightning, and his raiment white as snow: and for fear of him the keepers did shake, and became as dead" (Matthew 28:2 — 4). While they were in this unconscious state, it would appear, the revived Jesus was able to make his exit from the tomb without being observed.

Later, some of the watchmen went to Jerusalem to report to the Jewish authorities what had happened. The chief priests, Sadducean sceptics though they were, seemed to swallow the tall story, and simply bribed the men to declare that the disciples of Jesus had come during the night while they were asleep and had stolen his body.

The creator of this fantasy also was responsible for claiming another earthquake when Jesus expired, which also opened tombs and quickened the bodies of many saints, who afterwards went into Jerusalem and appeared to many people (Matthew 27:50 — 53. We cannot, therefore, place much reliance on such an imaginative writer anxious to rebut a cogent argument.

In considering the evidence for resurrection, we have already established that the followers of Jesus had no expectation that he would be raised from the dead and did not recall that he had made any reference to it in his lifetime. Had it been otherwise, they would have had no reason to mourn his death or trouble about the interment anointing of his corpse. The sayings of Jesus we find, which have him speak of his death and resurrection in advance, evidently were created as part of Christian propaganda as it was subsequently developed. Therefore, there was no call for the apostles to steal the body to justify a prediction of which they were not aware.

If the disciples were ignorant that Jesus had prophesied these experiences, much more so were his opponents. He had never told them, as Matthew alleges, "After three days I will rise again." In John, when the Jews ask for a sign, Jesus tells them that if they destroy this temple he will raise it up in three days. Only the author comments that Jesus meant his own body as the temple. He states clearly that the Jews thought Jesus was speaking of the building at Jerusalem. It was one of the accusations against Jesus before the chief priests that he had threatened to destroy the temple and miraculously rebuild it in three days (Mark 14:58). But it was not inferred that Jesus meant anything other than the physical temple built of stone.

The only other reference to the three days in relation to the

Resurrection is in the same Gospel that relates the story of the guard at the tomb. When Jesus was preaching in Galilee, the Pharisees asked him for a sign, to which he replied that their evil generation would get no sign except that of the prophet Jonah (Matthew 12:38 – 41). From the parallel in Luke 11:29 – 30, it is evident that Jesus is referring to Jonah's call to the Ninevites to repent. But Matthew singularly inserts a different interpretation: "As Jonah was three days and three nights in the whale's belly (Jonah 1:17); so shall the Son of Man be three days and three nights in the heart of the earth."

This is not very apt on Matthew's part, because he indicates that Jesus was in the tomb only one night and part of a second. More to the point, but not used in the Gospel, is a passage in Hosea: "Come, and let us return unto the Lord: for he hath torn, and he will heal us; for he hath smitten, and he will bind us up. After two days will he revive us: in the third day he will raise us up, and we shall live in his sight" (Hosea 6:1–2). After three days, apparently, revival would not be possible except by a miracle. Such a miracle was demanded in the case of Lazarus, according to John, who was resurrected on the fourth day, after decomposition had started.

Incredibly in Matthew's tale, the Roman governor Pontius Pilate was involved in what happened after the entombment of Jesus, since the chief priests and Pharisees went to him (on the Sabbath and first day of Passover!) and wanted him to have the tomb guarded to prevent the disciples from stealing the body by night and pretending Jesus had risen from the dead. Pilate so far concurs as to instruct them to employ their own guard to achieve maximum security. The tomb was sealed and the guard was posted, but the precautions were all in vain, as we have described. The soldiers were bribed by the chief priests to admit to Pilate, should he hear of the empty tomb, that the disciples had stolen the body of Jesus while they slept at their posts. One can hardly imagine Pilate, since he had been approached, failing to inquire into the matter fairly thoroughly. After all, it was he who had allowed Joseph of Arimathaea to receive the body of Jesus for burial. Furthermore, the theft of a corpse was a criminal offense. The guards concerned would have been lucky if they were not executed for their negligence, and the disciples would have been arrested and tortured to procure their confession.

The view that the apostles were the thieves, if it was ever seriously put forward, must be negatived. That is clear. But if it was a case of theft, who else would be interested in stealing the body? Well, there were grave-robbers. Usually, they would be seeking previous objects placed in the tomb with the dead, and they would not remove the corpse. But some robbers had a more sinister purpose: to traffic in human remains for medical or magical use. Relics of the crucified king of the Jews would be a tempting prize.

At this stage, we cannot rule out altogether that robbers broke into the tomb at night and made off with the body. But it does seem highly improbable. First, because it would mean taking a very great risk of discovery at a time when the whole nearby area was crowded with the tents of Passover pilgrims; and, second, because it is hardly credible that Jews would have been involved in such an enterprise.

It is much more likely that, if the body was removed as the women first believed, it would have been due to some pressing and wholly honorable reason. Any sceptic, however, invited to accept the Resurrection, most probably would react in the same way as the women in the first instance. He would propose that the body of Jesus had been extracted by human hands, possibly those of the friends of the deceased.

The preaching of the Resurrection did not begin to concern the Romans until a risk arose of imperial security being affected by messianic subversive activities; but this was not until the reign of the Emperor Claudius (41 — 54 a.d.). It has been suggested that an edict discovered at Nazareth in 1870 and dating from the Claudian period may have something to do with the matter. The text, inscribed in Latin on a marble slab, reads:

> *Ordinance of Caesar. It is my pleasure that graves and tombs remain undisturbed in perpetuity for those who have made them for the cult of their ancestors or children or members of their house. If, however, any man lay information that another has either demolished them, or has in any way extracted the buried or has maliciously transferred them to*

other places in order to wrong them, or has displaced the sealing or other stones, against such a one I order that a trial be instituted, as in respect of the gods, so in regard to the cult of mortals. For it shall be much more obligatory to honor the buried. Let it be absolutely forbidden for anyone to destroy them. In case of contravention I desire that the offender be sentenced to capital punishment on charge of violation of sepulture.

It is, of course, pure speculation that this edict was in any way prompted by the case of Jesus. But at least it illustrates Roman respect for the dead and abhorrence of the crime of despoliation of tombs.

7
The Gardener

On the basis of John's Gospel, the removal of Jesus' body might conceivably be attributed to a specific individual rather than to a number of persons. A gardener is introduced in the vicinity of the tomb, and John later describes Mary Magdalene as mistaking the risen Jesus for this gardener. She says to him, "Sir, if thou have borne him hence, tell me where thou hast laid him, and I will take him away."

John is the only one of the four Evangelists to mention that the body of Jesus was laid in a tomb located in a garden close to the place of execution. By garden we understand a plantation for fruit and vegetables, which would have a man in charge who in all probability would occupy a hut on the property. Since the place of crucifixion was on a hill, and Jerusalem itself was some 2,600 feet above sea level, the garden site was on high ground and would need to be shielded from the winds to protect the crops. We may infer, therefore, that at least on one side of the plantation there was a wall of natural rock in which one or more tombs had been hollowed out, perhaps utilizing an already existing cave. The tomb in question is said to have been a new one, and had not previously been used until Jesus was brought there.

It is commonly assumed that the property belonged to Joseph of Arimathaea, because this Jewish senator's estate was conveniently located nearby. It contained an unused tomb, and time was pressing for a burial because the Sabbath would commence at sunset. Actually, only Matthew claims that the tomb was Joseph's own, constructed for himself (Matthew 27:60).

From about the middle of the second century, however, the *Gospel of Peter*, in a manuscript fragment on the Passion, speaks of the sepulchre being in "the Garden of Joseph." In this uncanonical Gospel, it is the Jewish authorities who hand over the body of Jesus to Joseph of Arimathaea, not the Roman governor.

Let us assume for the present that the garden and tomb were Joseph's, and the gardener was in his employment. In that case, why would the gardener remove the corpse from the tomb when his own master had ceremoniously laid it there? Did he think he was acting in his master's interests, for he certainly was taking a risk?

Tradition and controversy are found contributing towards a possible explanation. The *Gospel of Peter* states that on the Sabbath, the day following the crucifixion, multitudes from Jerusalem and the surrounding regions came to see the sepulchre. This possibility is likely enough, since the execution of Jesus, whether he was regarded as a prophet or claimant to the Jewish throne, must have greatly stirred and shocked multitudes of Jews at Jerusalem, both native and foreign, assembled for the feast of Unleavened Bread. They could at least show sympathy and respect, and not merely curiosity, by visiting the sepulchre. Some went, no doubt, to weep and pray there. The spot was clearly within the range of a Sabbath Day's journey on foot.

In these crowds, the Church Father Tertullian, or a source he used, saw a reason for the action attributed to the gardener. Tertullian, it is written, rejoices at the fiery fate of the Jews at the Last Judgment, and in imagination he mocks them for their treatment of Jesus. "This is he," I shall say, "the son of the carpenter or the harlot, the Sabbath-breaker, the Samaritan, who had a devil." And he concludes, "This is he whom the disciples secretly stole away, that it might be said he had risen—unless it was the gardener who removed him, lest his lettuces should be trampled by the throng of visitors!" (*De Spectaculis*, 30, translated by T. R. Glover, Loeb Classical Library).

So in the clash of argument about the empty tomb, we have another suggestion on the Jewish side arising from early Christian sources, that the gardener had acted on his own initiative to save his master's crops. It is not very convincing and indeed not worth entertaining, since the crowds would be even more anxious to stare at the empty tomb. Neither is it likely that the gardener would assume so much personal responsibility, since his master had intentionally laid the body of Jesus in his private sepulchre.

But we have not finished with the gardener, for both Christian and Jewish legend has been busy with him.

In the British Museum (Orient. MSS. 6804) is a Coptic manuscript entitled *The Book of the Resurrection*, attributed to the Apostle Bartholomew. In this document the Jews, after the crucifixion, are looking for a safe place to deposit the body of Jesus so the disciples will not steal it secretly. A gardener, named Philogenes, tells them: "There is a tomb quite close to my vegetable garden; bring him, lay him in it, and I myself will keep watch over him." The Jews accept, but it is the intention of the gardener, when the Jews have departed, to take away the body of Jesus and anoint it for burial, presumably elsewhere. When Philogenes goes to the tomb at midnight, however, he finds it occupied by angels and God raises Jesus from the dead.

This text builds up the part of the gardener in a favorable sense. He intends to remove the body of Jesus to defeat the aim of the Jews, which was to prevent the disciples from knowing where he was entombed.

On both sides of the controversy, an actual gardener and his vegetable garden figure in the legends and traditions, and furnish opportunity for alternative explanations of the empty tomb. The probability is that John's Gospel gave rise to the gardener and his garden being brought into the argument, which continued in controversy between Jews and Christians over many centuries. But there does remain the faint possibility that some genuine additional piece of information was in circulation.

We have quoted Tertullian on a Jewish suggestion that the gardener removed the body of Jesus to save his crop of lettuce from the feet of the crowds who came to see the tomb. The crowds also are mentioned in the *Gospel of Peter*. So it is likely that Tertullian's information came directly or indirectly from a written source.

When the Gospels—not only the canonical ones—were composed and put into circulation, Christian polemics and missionary activity assured that some of them would become known in Jewish circles. Some evidence exists of this Gospel material in rabbinical literature in the form of allusions, several of which relate to the experiences of persons living in the latter part of the first century A.D. In particular, those Gospels that were available in Hebrew or Aramaic would be more familiar to Jews.

Certainly by the second century there were uncanonical Gospels of this nature in circulation, emanating from the (*Notsrim*) Nazoreans (Jewish believers in Jesus as Messiah) and their offshoots. Such Gospels—e.g., that known as the *Gospel of the Hebrews*—are as yet only accessible in relatively late quotations, none of which cover the circumstances we are considering. *Hebrews* did record the appearance of the risen Jesus to his brother Jacob (James), referred to by Paul (1 Corinthians 15:7).

I have long held that this Gospel (see my book, *According to the Hebrews*, 1937) prompted the creation of various Jewish counter-Gospels, which were parodies or caricatures familiar to Christian authorities in the Middle Ages. The most prominent of these was often entitled *Toldoth Jeshu* ("Generations of Jesus;" compare Matthew 1:1). It is in this material, designed primarily to sustain Jews in their resistance to the blandishments and threats of Christianity, that we find what had been inherited and worked upon from Tertullian's time, and even earlier.

From Lyons (the Roman *Lugdunum*) in the ninth century, two references have reached us. One is from the archbishop Amulo in his *Epistola, Seu Liber contra Judaeos, ad Carolum Regem* (ca. 847), where he declares on Jewish authority that Jesus had been taken down hastily from the tree on which he had been hanged, and that they "thrust him into a tomb in a certain garden full of cabbages (*caulibus pleno*), so that their land should not be contaminated."

In another *Epistola*, by Amulo's predecessor, Agobard, *De Judaici Superstitionibus* (ca. 826), the author cites the teachings of the Jewish elders who set down in writing that after Jesus was hanged, "he was buried by a canal, and handed over to a certain Jew to guard. By night, however, he was carried away by the sudden overflowing of the canal, and though he was sought for twelve months by the order of Pilate, he could never be found."

We have quoted only pertinent sentences from each of these sources; but from the contexts it is evident that the information was derived, not necessarily directly, from *Toldoth* manuscripts. Elements in this material were already of high antiquity in the ninth century, reflecting a line of tradition relating to the garden burial of Jesus and to the gardener. Much in the intervening centuries had become more fanciful both in Christian and Jewish apocrypha, sometimes combined, but a grain of truth could have been preserved. By Agobard's "canal" we are to understand an irrigation channel serving the plantation or vegetable plot, a very appropriate feature.

When we turn to a representative text of the *Toldoth Jeshu*, the Hebrew Codex in the University Library of Strasburg entitled *The History of Jesus the Nazarene*, we find an alternative version of the part played by the gardener. The Jewish authorities were at a loss to explain that the body of Jesus was not where it was buried, and his disciples were claiming that he had risen from the dead and ascended to heaven. What the Jewish elders did not know was that "a certain man had taken him forth from his grave and brought him into his garden, and had divided (*alt.,* stopped up) the waters that were flowing into his garden, and had digged in the sand and buried him, and had brought back the waters into their channel over the grave." The garden keeper later reveals what he had done, claiming that he had acted to thwart any design of the disciples to steal the body themselves.

Basically, the Jewish suggestions of what happened after Jesus' entombment are no more fanciful than what the Gospels, especially Matthew, describe. From their respective standpoints, both seek to account for a mutually agreed fact: that the body of Jesus was missing. The Gospels do so in a miraculous manner, while the Jewish protagonists offer conceivable natural explanations, seizing particularly on the gardener as a key figure. What is adduced from the Jewish side, however, is no more authoritative and convincing than what the Gospels convey. We are in an atmosphere of controversy and propaganda rather than of reality.

We should note in passing that it has not been determined by any means that the plantation's gardener was involved. In Mark, the man seen by the women was robed in white, unlikely raiment for a gardener, while the figure seen by Mary Magdalene, according to John, was only *thought* by her to be the gardener. He reveals himself as Jesus in the story, but Mary may well have seen someone else.

There is something else that calls for consideration, if there were circumstances which lend it probability: that the body of Jesus, for valid and imperative reasons, was transferred from the initial tomb to another place of burial.

8
Joseph of Arimathaea

We turn from the supposed gardener to Joseph of Arimathaea, identified by tradition as the owner of the property in which was located the tomb where Jesus was placed. Joseph is one of those personalities in the Gospels who arrives on the scene at a psychological moment, plays his part, and is not heard of again in the biblical records. He is an individual of note, a member of the Jewish Government of Judea under the Romans, by religious affiliation a Pharisee or near-Pharisee. Matthew goes so far as to say that he was a disciple of Jesus, which John qualifies by intimating that this association was secret "for fear of the Jews."

According to John, Joseph of Arimathaea would appear to have been in the confidence of another Jewish counsellor, Nicodemus, who had once paid a visit to Jesus at night to learn more about him and his teaching. Only John mentions Nicodemus as associated with Joseph in the entombment of the body of Jesus, and this may be a courtesy mention on the author's part as a way of paying a personal tribute to Nicodemus for speaking on behalf of Jesus before the Jewish Council (John 7:50 – 52). The other Gospel writers do not seem to know of Nicodemus in this connection or any other.

Because of the limited information available to the Evangelists, it appears they were not in a position to amplify upon references in their sources when it was badly needed. Some of them come up with accounts of such tremendous consequence—such as the raising of Lazarus and the guard posted at the tomb in which Jesus lay—that they could not have been omitted by the other disciples had they known about them.

Sometimes we can perceive a motive for the introduction of novelties. They support claims or counter objections. But others appear to derive from genuine memories and traditions, and convey not only how much more might have been told if sufficient records had been made and preserved, but that such material might well have given us a very different image of the activities of Jesus and the circumstances relating to him. Even with the Gospels as they have come down to us, there are traces of hidden history in statements that are not especially brought to our attention, the significance of which was evidently overlooked. We should be the most wary of what is thrust under our noses, so to speak. Accordingly, we have to wrestle with the problem of distinguishing between motivated and unmotivated material, and with what each implies in fact or fiction.

The impression given of a Jewish Council at Jerusalem that was wholly hostile to Jesus is clearly at variance with information that at least two of its members (and there were probably a number of others) were defenders of Jesus, and some possibly accepted him as the Messiah. John's Gospel tells us that the "Dear Disciple" was known to the high priest, so it is evident that Jesus was in a position to learn directly and indirectly of the Council's views and intentions and make his dispositions accordingly. We are not informed that Joseph of Arimathaea had personally met Jesus, but there is no reason why he, just as much as Nicodemus, should not have had private discussion with him.

Before we consider Joseph further, we need to be clear about what the Gospels have to say about him and his actions. Among other things, it is important to investigate whether the refer-

ences to him could have had any other motivation than recording a matter of interest.

Mark, the earliest of the four Gospels, gives very straightforward information. Jesus died on the cross shortly after 1500
hours on Friday afternoon, some three hours before sunset
when the Jewish Sabbath would commence. Because it was the
eve of the Sabbath, "Joseph of Arimathaea, an honorable coun-
selor, who also waited for the Kingdom of God, came, and
went in boldly to Pilate, and craved the body of Jesus." The
governor was amazed to hear that Jesus was already dead—he
had been on the cross not much more than six hours—and
summoned the centurion in charge of the execution. The centurion confirmed that Jesus was indeed dead, and thereupon
Pilate allowed Joseph to have his body for burial. Joseph went
off to buy fine linen, then took Jesus down from the cross,
swathed him in the linen, laid him in a rock-hewn tomb, and
rolled a stone across the entrance.

Joseph, according to Mark, was a member of the Jewish
Council, and therefore well-informed of what had transpired
concerning Jesus; he also was a man of good Pharisee type.
Nothing is said of his having any special association with Jesus.
As it was near the Sabbath, he determined, if possible, to give
Jesus a decent burial as a pious act and mark of respect. He had
the courage to appeal to Pilate for the corpse; but the statement
that he only went to buy linen afterwards, for use as a winding
sheet, suggests that he was not too sure in advance of the
outcome of his request. The account is the kind that would
appeal to Roman piety, and Mark is believed to have composed
his Gospel in Italy. Joseph acted by himself throughout, and it is
not said that the tomb used for the burial actually belonged
to him.

Matthew and Luke seem to be based on Mark or a common
source. Where they agree against Mark is in omitting reference
to Pilate's inquiry as to whether Jesus was in fact dead. Matthew
makes Joseph a wealthy man and disciple. Joseph does not go
to buy linen, and could be presumed to have had it in advance;
finally, the tomb is a new one made by Joseph for himself. Luke

points out that Joseph had been no party to the design and action of the Jewish Council against Jesus. The tomb, in Luke also, was a new one, though he does not say it was Joseph's own, and he stresses that the tomb had had no previous occupant.

With slight variations, the references to Joseph in the first three Gospels represent a narration of brief extent, not found practicable to expand upon authoritatively. The differences are in the nature of individual touches, and do not derive from independent traditions. When the so-called Synoptic Gospels were composed, John the Priest had not yet told his story, declared when published to be that of an eyewitness.

John's record is not merely a fourth employment of the same basic material; it supplements and diverges from it strikingly. It could be an approach from personal knowledge meant to be more circumstantial, but on the other hand it also could possibly have a different motivation.

Before turning to John, let us consider the motivation of the Markan tradition. Was the Joseph episode only designed to put on record a notable act of charity by an individual well-disposed towards Jesus, and to exhibit the Roman governor not in an unfriendly light? The interposition of Joseph of Arimathaea, if factual, deserved to be set down, and all the more for the reasons suggested. But, additionally, there could be another less obvious aim.

When considered carefully, the intervention of Joseph was of vital consequence to the resurrection thesis. Had he not appeared on the scene at a psychological moment, or had he failed in his laudable mission, the circumstances would have been most unfavorable to resurrection and might even be thought to render it impossible.

Jesus was crucified with two others, and the lives of all of them would have been ended—as John points out—before the beginning of the Sabbath at sunset, since in Jewish law (Deuteronomy 21:23) the bodies of the hanged must be taken down and buried before nightfall. The Romans apparently respected this ruling and, in conformity with it, the deaths of the crucified were expedited by the Roman method of breaking their legs. But what would then have happened to the bodies? In such serious criminal cases, a hole would have been dug in the ground and the three corpses cast into a common grave.

How could one of these bodies, consigned to imprisoning and suffocating dust, be singled out specially to be raised from the dead, leaving the other two behind? Surely it was requisite that the corpse of Jesus must not undergo the fate of the others! This could be secured only if his body quite distinctively could come into friendly hands. Joseph of Arimathaea, therefore, played a vital part in the resurrection story by seeking to obtain possession of Jesus' body, an endeavor in which he succeeded. Jesus, unlike his fellow sufferers, was spared interment in the earth by being placed in a cool ventilated tomb *above ground*, which was conveniently at hand. His wounded limbs were bandaged with the clean linen Joseph had brought. There could be no confusion with other bodies to complicate the resurrection, since the tomb was new and contained no other occupant. All the details of the Joseph story were necessary if Jesus was to appear again alive from the dead, and they may well be thought to exceed pure chance.

Reference to the actions of Joseph, then, has more to it than the recording of a charitable deed by an eminent and courageous man. It is tacitly acknowledged that for purposes of faith in the resurrection of Jesus, it had to be recorded how his body came to be distinctively preserved.

One point, however, was overlooked by Mark. If Joseph, in petitioning Pilate for the body, was acting virtually on the spur of the moment, how did he know where he would take it if his request was granted? What reason would he have for certitude that in the vicinity of the place of execution an unused tomb would be available. Of all the Evangelists, only Matthew noted the difficulty and made the necessary correction. Prior knowledge of the tomb presented no problem, since it was Joseph's own, newly constructed for his eventual demise.

Was this true, however, or did Matthew invent it to meet objections? One would expect John especially to have this information, but he does not give it. He says: "Now in the place where he [Jesus] was crucified there was a garden; and in the garden a new sepulchre, wherein was never man yet laid. There laid they Jesus therefore because of the Jews' preparation day; for the sepulchre was nigh at hand" (John 19:41–42).

There remains the possibility that both the garden and the sepulchre were Joseph's, but the evidence is not conclusive. Even if they were not his, however, he must have known of them. In either case, Joseph's action probably was not as spontaneous as it was made to appear. It might well have formed part of a premeditated plan, facilitated by prior awareness of the unused tomb's proximity.

There is a related question. John conveys that the tomb in the garden was utilized because it was so close to the place of execution. Clearly, time was pressing because of the imminence of the Sabbath, and the body could not be taken any great distance. This factor is also indicated by Luke. We do not meet with the suggestion that the tomb was intended to be the permanent resting-place of the remains of Jesus. It could have been Joseph's purpose early in the new week to remove the body officially to another tomb.

The women of Jesus' company who had witnessed the crucifixion had carefully marked the position of the tomb to which he had been taken. When they brought their spices there around dawn on Sunday morning, their alarm was natural when they found the tomb open and the body gone. They may well have anticipated that Jesus would be taken to another tomb subsequently, and in all probability in broad daylight. They might expect to know about this possibility because it would not be completely hushed up. But now, as was evident and totally unexpected, the removal obviously had taken place during the night after the termination of the Sabbath, and there was no immediate way of learning where the body was. They rushed back to Peter with the unhappy news, "They have taken away the Master out of the sepulchre, and we don't know where they have put him." "They" in this context of John's Gospel presumably refers to Joseph of Arimathaea and Nicodemus, though it could refer to foes of Jesus.

There is decidedly room in the sources for the impression that the tomb was never intended by Joseph and his associates to become Jesus' permanent resting place. It was immediately

convenient and the Sabbath was at hand. This temporary interment would have been understood by the disciples, and a
change of tomb later would have been acceptable to them. But
nothing seemed to call for the urgency of the body's secret
removal in the night after the sabbath had ended. It was what
the women found when they arrived at dawn on Sunday morning that was both wholly unexpected and, under the circumstances, conceivably sinister. They did not stay to question
the man they found at the now empty tomb, and took to their
heels in alarm.

We have observed that Joseph's intervention was necessary to
prevent the burial of Jesus' corpse in the ground with his
fellow-sufferers, an obstacle to the resurrection thesis. In the
eyewitness account in John, we have Joseph being assisted by
Nicodemus, of whom the Synoptic writers knew nothing. And,
certainly, Joseph must have had one or more helpers to take
down the body, convey it to the neighboring tomb, and close its
entrance with the massive stone.

But John also introduces another significant incident. Not
only was the body of Jesus kept out of the ground and away
from the two others who had been crucified: his limbs were
preserved intact, while their legs had been broken to expedite
death. Jesus escaped the *crurifragium* because he was deemed
to be already dead when the soldiers came with their mallets.
Instead, to make sure Jesus had expired, one of them pierced
his side with a spear. John claims that Old Testament prophecies thus were fulfilled; but we may also see that another serious
impediment to acceptance of the resurrection was removed:
Jesus would not be reanimated as a cripple, unable to move
about freely.

9
Another Possibility

We must chalk up a question mark regarding the garden tomb and its owner. The evidence is inconclusive that the garden and the tomb belonged to Joseph of Arimathaea and, therefore, we cannot know for certain whether the gardener was employed by him. There are both Christian and Jewish stories—polemical and apologetic—that present the gardener as acting on his own initiative (see Chapter 7). It is not possible to clarify whether he played any part at all in what took place. The stories could have originated simply because in John's Gospel, Mary Magdalene saw a man near the tomb, supposed him to be a gardener, and asked him if he had removed the body of Jesus from the sepulchre. In the Gospel, the man proves to be the risen Jesus; but he could have been someone else, conceivably the young man who Mark says the women saw at the tomb.

Our foundation material is that there was a vacant tomb close to the place of crucifixion, that it was in a garden where fruit and vegetables were grown, and it probably was cut into a natural wall of rock. This tomb was used to house the body of Jesus because of its proximity, and because little time was left before the commencement of the Sabbath. Three crucial questions arise:

(1) If the tomb was not Joseph's, how did he know it was there and available?
(2) Was it his intention to remove the body later to a more permanent resting place?
(3) By whom, and for what reason, was the body taken from the tomb during the night following the Sabbath?

Dealing with the first question, it is difficult to understand why Joseph of Arimathaea should have gone to Pilate so belatedly with a petition to be given the body of Jesus if he did not know where he was going to deposit it. There wasn't enough time to hunt for a tomb, or transport the body any great distance. At least a house could have been used, or some protected place in which the body could lie temporarily without being disturbed. Consequently, it seems very dubious that Joseph acted on a sudden impulse in going to the governor, having had no prior intention to gain possession of the body. We must infer that, regardless of whether he owned the tomb, he must have known about its existence and availability. If the tomb was definitely not his, he either had previously been told about it or had been over the ground and discovered it. Whichever was true, it suggests that a plan requiring control over the fate of the body of Jesus had been formed in advance of the crucifixion. This is a very important deduction.

Regarding the second question, if John's account of what took place is based on eye-witness information, it is clearly to be preferred to that of Matthew. John definitely states that the body of Jesus was deposited in the convenient tomb "because of the Jews' preparation day; for the sepulchre was nigh at hand." We would then have to say that there is a strong possibility that the tomb was used out of temporary necessity, and there could have been the intention to remove the body later on to a permanent resting place. This possibility could be true even if the tomb had belonged to Joseph and had been designed for his own remains. It is unlikely that he would feel it fitting that the tomb in due course should be shared by himself and conceivably members of his family. For a permanent resting place, either another tomb would have to be prepared as soon as practicable to house Jesus alone, or Joseph would wish to construct another for his domestic use. On the other hand, as we shall see, there may have been a design to remove the body for another purpose entirely, which will be considered in dealing with the third question.

We can appreciate that if the body of Jesus were to be transferred to a different tomb, it would be done as soon as practicable, partly because of the onset of decomposition. It certainly might be politic to carry out the transfer privately at night, in view of the possibility of a popular demonstration or disturbance, or official objection. But for what reason would the movement have to be the very next night?

This brings us to our third question. There does not appear to be any likelihood in this instance that either the Romans or grave-robbers were responsible for opening the tomb and removing the body, and certainly we may exonerate the apostles. There is also a significant urgency about the proceedings, which does not point to the gardener, if involved, as the prime mover. It seems much more probable that the man responsible for the removal of the body of Jesus that Saturday night was the courageous man who had "boldly" gone to Pilate to ask for it the previous evening. This man, Joseph of Arimathaea, as we have indicated, must have had knowledge of the proximity and availability of the garden tomb prior to the crucifixion of Jesus. If a reason is to be sought for the removal of the body so very quickly from its resting place, a cogent one—and it is no new one—presents itself: an attempt was being made to save Jesus. Such an attempt would have to have been planned in advance.

Let us go over what was demanded if success were to be achieved. The torture of crucifixion normally lasted several days. The time Jesus spent on the cross, therefore, had to be greatly reduced. Because Jesus was not tried by Pilate before Friday morning, he could not be condemned and crucified until later in the day. Since his body must be taken down from the cross before sunset, his torment could only last a few hours, insufficient to kill him in ordinary circumstances. Neither of those who were crucified with Jesus at the same time is said to have succumbed.

Then it had to be assured to the extent possible that his body should remain whole, avoiding the inevitability of immediate death which would have resulted from the breaking of his legs.

Therefore, before the *crurifragium* was applied, it was essential that Jesus would have to present the appearance of being already dead. It is reported that just before he "died" he was given a drink from a sponge filled with vinegar. This could have been suitably drugged. In John's Gospel it is said that Jesus deliberately called out for this drink when he knew "that all things were now accomplished" (John 19:28). In addition, Jesus had to be saved from being summarily interred with his fellow-sufferers, which would have rendered his recovery impossible and even prevented access to his body. Here we have Joseph's intervention with Pilate to gain possession of the body.

Now it became a question, despite the unexpected spear-thrust by a Roman soldier, of preserving life in Jesus. Joseph brought clean linen and Nicodemus furnished spices, which would bandage the wounds effectively and prevent infection. The body was conveyed to the known adjacent tomb cut into the cool rock, where it was to remain until the end of the Sabbath. If Jesus still had life in him, as the blood from the spear-wound would suggest, he would nevertheless be unconscious for many hours. Such a state would be inevitable after prolonged sleeplessness, flogging, the effects of crucifixion, and, we might add, the contribution of a drug.

The success of such a rescue operation would depend on speedy medical help. Therefore, Jesus had to be brought out of the tomb at the earliest possible moment after the termination of the Sabbath. And because such a rescue was a serious criminal act designed to defeat the ends of justice, this removal had to take place after dark. The open tomb, the removed and folded linen bandages, and the disappearance of the body before dawn on Sunday would all have a natural explanation if it was intended to restore Jesus to health and activity by taking him where he would receive care and treatment.

All the elements we have listed fit the most reliable and consistent features of the available traditions, and they enable us to discard the idea that the body of Jesus was hastily taken from one tomb to place it in another. We might wonder, however, whether such a plan would have a chance of success were it not for an incident described by the Jewish historian Josephus. In his *Autobiography*, Josephus relates that after the

capture of Jerusalem in 70 A.D. he was engaged on an errand
for the Roman commander Titus when he came across three
crosses on which three of his acquaintances had been crucified.
Greatly upset, he went to Titus and begged for their lives. His
petition was granted. The men were taken down, their wounds
dressed, and every effort was made by the doctors to save them.
Two of the men succumbed, but one was healed and survived,
which showed that recovery from crucifixion was possible,
especially if the victim had not suffered for many hours. The
more favorable the circumstances, the better the prospects. All
the conditions were conducive to success in securing the survi-
val of Jesus except the spear-wound, referred to only in John's
Gospel in terms of fulfillment of prophesy. Some of these conditions strongly suggest prior planning, as we have noted.

Regarding medical care, the most skilled Jewish physicians of
the time were the Essenes, who, like Joseph of Arimathaca,
awaited the coming of the Kingdom of God and held strong
Messianic beliefs based on the interpretation of the Hebrew
Scriptures. Josephus reports on their knowledge of the medici-
nal properties of herbs, and they claimed that their art had been
handed down from Shem the son of Noah. Josephus also mentions that they dressed in white robes. According to Mark, when
the women of Jesus' company arrived at the tomb on Sunday
morning and found it open, they encountered a young man
dressed in white who spoke to them.

Since the recovery of the Dead Sea Scrolls, we have gained
more knowledge of the Essenes' opposition to the Roman government and to the Jewish chief priests. In addition, it has
become more evident that there was a relationship between the
Essenes and the primitive Christians.

The suggestion is by no means new that the crucified Christ
was ministered to by Essenes, and it seems extremely likely that
the services of one or two of them were enlisted, both to provide
the drug that would make it appear that he died on the cross
and to contribute their skill to his recovery. What does not
follow is that Jesus made such a miraculous return to health
that he was able almost immediately to appear to his disciples,
and that this explains the accounts of his resurrection. Some
writers have appreciated this, and would have Jesus slowly

nursed back to health unknown to his disciples, a theory which necessitates that he must have remained in the world somewhere.

In this case, it has to be presumed that Jesus had abandoned his Messianic claims and left his disciples to their fate, still believing what he was personally in a position to demonstrate was a lie. One legend would have him go to India and be buried there. It is conceivable, of course, that in his ordeal on the cross Jesus suffered some brain damage, and thus mentally lost contact with his former life and activities. He might have lived on, oblivious of his previous associations.

Theories to this effect cannot be disproved. But the Gospels may discredit their validity by recounting the presence of a man at the empty tomb, ready and apparently anxious to give the disciples some explanatory and reassuring message. If we accept this man as one of the Essene fraternity involved in the attempt to save Jesus, we must believe that he evidently had no reason to doubt that Jesus was still alive and receiving attention wherever he had been taken. He could not know positively, however, that the ministrations of his colleagues would be successful.

We might then postulate that Jesus did recover consciousness not long after he had been conveyed to some suitable place for treatment, and that his first thought was for the sorrow of his followers who believed him to be dead. He would certainly wish to get word to them that he was alive. Resurrection does not apply here, since Jesus had not in fact died. Later, of course, he could have had a relapse and expired.

We reach an initial conclusion, then, that there was nothing miraculous about the tomb being empty on the Sunday morning. The explanation of resurrection came as an inspiration of John the Priest when he visited the tomb with Peter. The series of previous events points most circumstantially to a design involving high-up Jewish friends of Jesus. At least one of them, Joseph of Arimathaea, was intimately and specifically involved at great personal risk to save him from extinction. The manner of the operation had been devised in advance without the cognizance of the Galilean apostles. It was necessary for the plan to

remain highly secret so there would be no riot or public disturbance in which many might have been killed, and so that there
was no prevention of the execution of the sentence called for by
Roman law. Had the plan not been kept very secret, there was
also the risk that one of Jesus' not-very-bright followers would
have learned of it and given it away in some thought-
less manner.

It was a bold and, by no means, unpracticable plan. But who
had originated it? Was it Joseph of Arimathaea and one or two
others, such as Nicodemus? And what of Jesus? Had he expected to find himself alive again, or was he taken by surprise?

If Joseph of Arimathaea was the originator of the design, he
would have needed to know many things in advance. The first
would be that Jesus was going to be crucified by the Romans.
This might be deduced from inside information of the Jewish
Council's intention to hand Jesus over to the governor Pontius
Pilate, and from the fact that Jesus, when he had ridden into
Jerusalem, had accepted acclaim by the populace as king of the
Jews, thus making himself liable to the charge of high treason
against the Roman emperor. Also, Joseph possibly might have
been apprised of references Jesus had made to the fate awaiting
him. The action of Judas, in coming to the council with his offer
of betrayal, would have conveyed that fate as imminent.

But all the information Joseph might be credited with acquir-
ing would allow only certain ingredients of a plan to be formulated sufficiently far ahead. What could not positively be known
sufficiently in advance was that Jesus would be convicted and
executed on the eve of the Sabbath at the commencement of the
Feast of Unleavened Bread. Without this vital knowledge, the
shaping of a clear-cut design was out of the question. The chief
constituents of the plan were contingent on prior awareness of
a march of events related to important time factors. Their character was dictated by such awareness.

We are dealing with a very carefully devised scheme; not one
that was fortuitous. Preparations were involved to meet a particular set of circumstances, which demanded some knowledge
beyond the competence of Joseph of Arimathaea to ascertain if
he was acting on his own initiative. He must have been promp-

ted by someone who was in a key position to program developments. Bizarre as it may seem, there was only one such person, Jesus himself.

We are now, therefore, forced to look at Jesus in a new way—not as the victim of adverse and hostile forces, but as the master and planner of his own destiny. The Dear Disciple wants us to look at him in such a way, in making him say that he lays down his own life, so that he may take it back. "No man taketh it from me, but I lay it down of myself. I have power to lay it down, and I have the power to take it again" (John 10:17–18). It would come as no surprise to Jesus to find himself alive, released from the cross, because this was what he had designed with the aid and cooperation of particular friends.

10
Christ Strategist

It would appear logical that a plan to save Jesus in the manner we have described could only be carried out with his knowledge and cooperation. It called for very careful advance planning affecting his movements and actions, as well as those of others. Indeed, if there were a plan, as we hope to demonstrate, we would have to propose Jesus himself as the author of it, since an initiative of such intricacy could hardly be credited to persons, however well-disposed, who had no overwhelming incentive.

To consider fairly such a startling proposition, we have to cease to be guided by the doctrines of the Christian faith; no easy matter for the believer. The Christian is accustomed to accept that what he believes about Jesus was also in the mind of Jesus. Therefore, Jesus must have been conscious of his divinity and assured that he would rise from the dead and return to the heaven from which he had descended, having completed the redemptive task which had called for his incarnation and death on the cross.

The Christian Christ, knowing all things and having the superhuman powers of deity, would be above the necessity for stratagems and plots to attain his ends. Our Jesus, however, is wholly human with a mind and will of his own and a distinctive personality and intelligence. He has to employ his wits to triumph over his adversaries.

When I presented the fresh interpretation of Jesus I had arrived at in my book, *The Passover Plot*, a sensation was created which has had enduring consequences. Insight was so much in line with evidential indications that for multitudes Jesus for the first time became real. And though thousands of Christians, chiefly fundamentalists, were shocked, they had no ammunition to counter my thesis except that of villification and misrepresentation. It was so clear that the book was not anti-Jesus but quite the contrary, and gave full weight to his conviction that he was the Messiah, that those who wanted to overcome its influence, as well as certain journalists who were out for a good story with banner press headlines, tended to concentrate on the issues affecting doctrines of the death and resurrection of Jesus.

The critics wished to make it appear that I had presented Jesus as a deceiver who had faked his death on the cross by means of a drug to delude his disciples into believing that he had risen from the dead. Needless to say, I had not stated or suggested anything of the kind. What I had set out to demonstrate was that Jesus believed he would have to suffer but not unto death, and consequently would triumph over his enemies without any requirement of resurrection. Because of the empty tomb, it was the Dear Disciple's inspired guess that Jesus had risen from the dead. Since the followers of Jesus, on the same authority, had not been expecting their Master's resurrection, he could not have had any intention to deceive them. One can appreciate how orthodox Christians stake their hope of immortality on faith in Christ's resurrection, and thus it is both alien to them and objectionable to remove this feature from their religious thinking.

Honest investigation, however, cannot be impeded, even if the results should turn out to be unwelcome. There is need, therefore, for me to explain my reasoning in greater detail in hope that a fairer judgment may lead to a reassessment that Christians can live with.

We have to begin by concentrating on Jesus as a man, with the mind of a man. The Gospels, though inevitably colored by the formulation of a doctrine of Christ, a Christology, nonetheless accentuate the humanity of Jesus. He hungers and thirsts, suffers pain and weariness, experiences joy and sorrow, and all human emotions. But he is also strongly individualistic with a quick-acting brain; he is masterful and determined, fertile in imagination, colorful in speech, sharp-witted, often with a biting tongue, enterprising, and resourceful. What is commonly called the public ministry of Jesus is, in fact, a purposeful, well-planned, and well-organized campaign. When we study his behavior and dispositions, we are able to pick up many intimations of his capacity which, if we do not apprehend him as a very skillful planner, we would be likely to miss.

Some of the things we need to observe have significance because of the political and social circumstances in Israel at the time, when the country was under Roman rule. We note, for example, that not until Jesus is on his way to Jerusalem for the last time does he allow himself publicly to be hailed as Messiah, son of David—that is, as the predestined king of the Jews—and he previously rejected having the people make him king. Had he done otherwise, his ministry would have been cut short by his prompt arrest and execution, since to be proclaimed king without Roman authority in a Roman province was high treason against Caesar.

When teaching in public about the New Society, the Kingdom of God to be established on earth, Jesus is careful to speak only in parables so as to give nothing away to spies and informers in the crowd. No less than five of the twelve envoys he chooses in Galilee are fishermen with boats, thus providing an emergency source of escape across the Sea of Galilee to the politically safer areas of the Gaulan and the Decapolis.

The fact of the matter is that we are habituated, by teaching and tradition, to regard Jesus as almost completely isolated from the grim realities that affected his people. We are primarily absorbed in spiritual and ethical issues. Consequently, we have not sufficiently considered his reactions to contemporary events, holding him to be representative of eternal values and verities. Now we have to be aware of him differently, and there is much for us to notice.

The movements and actions of Jesus are always intelligent and decisive. He makes his headquarters at the tactically important town of Capernaum. He sends out the twelve envoys (apostles) with explicit instructions. He defines his mission as confined to the lost sheep of the house of Israel, to bring them to repentance so that the Day of Redemption may come speedily. When this campaign meets with insufficent response, he "sets his face steadfastly to go to Jerusalem" to prepare for his individual act of atonement as Israel's king. This act is to take place at the Jewish freedom festival, the Passover, in the spring of the year; but the journey to Jerusalem just mentioned is at the festival of Tabernacles in the previous autumn. Uniquely, Jesus remains in Jerusalem for about three months. We have to ask why this was necessary.

The more carefully and objectively we look at what is related about Jesus in the context of contemporary conditions, and thinking of him specifically as a descendant of King David, claimant as Messiah to the Jewish throne, the more evident it seems that we are dealing with a man of very high I.Q. and tactical skill who is bringing to bear on his objectives the attributes of humanity—not deity. It comes as a revelation when we grasp that we are dealing with a mastermind on the earthly plane, a brilliant strategist whose calculated moves we can follow with keen appreciation.

But if we have yet to be convinced that Jesus is to be looked at in this light, let the Gospels provide confirmation.

The material furnished by the Gospels varies considerably in quality and reliability, as we should expect from their character and from the resources they could command. Their testimony is at its best where no theological or didactic purpose is being served, and where the writers do not appear to be conscious of the implication of what they put on record.

The most stirking and clear-cut example of a stratagem employed by Jesus involving secret dispositions concerns the arrangements for the Passover communal meal in Jerusalem before his arrest. The circumstances are related in Mark's Gospel and repeated almost verbatim in Luke. Matthew omits the details but shows himself aware of what Mark had reported. We will quote Mark in full.

The passage describes how Judas went to the chief priests with an offer to betray Jesus to them. At this time, Jesus and the apostles are at Bethany on the far side of the Mount of Olives east of Jerusalem.

> And the first day of unleavened bread, when they killed the passover [i.e. the paschal lamb], his disciples said unto him, "Where wilt thou that we go and prepare that thou mayest eat the passover?"
>
> And he sendeth forth two of his disciples, and said unto them, "Go ye into the city, and there shall meet you a man bearing a pitcher of water: follow him. And wheresoever he shall go in, say ye to the goodman of the house, The Master saith, 'Where is the guestchamber, where I shall eat the passover with my disciples?' And he will shew you a large upper room furnished and prepared: there make ready for us."
>
> And his disciples went forth, and came into the city, and found as he had said unto them: and they made ready the passover.
>
> And in the evening he cometh with the twelve (Mark 14:12–17).

Luke's account follows Mark's so closely that either he must have had Mark before him as he wrote, or both Evangelists used a common written source. What distinguishes Luke's record is that he names the two disciples Jesus sends to Jerusalem, they are two of his three intimates, Peter and John, son of Zebedae.

Matthew does not relate the circumstances of the rendezvous with the bearer of the pitcher of water. Jesus simply tells the disciples, "Go into the city to such a man, and say unto him, 'The Master saith, my time is at hand; I will keep the passover at thy house with my disciples.'" We do not know whether Matthew was merely abbreviating, or whether he did not like what the incident conveyed. However, he agrees with the others on one point. None of them appears to want to name the man in whom Jesus placed such confidence that he trusted him with his life. This is a remarkable fact in itself, and we shall return to the point later.

The essence of the story is that Jesus, without informing the closest of his followers, had privately and at some time in advance made plans to observe the Passover in Jerusalem in a manner that would not allow the hostile authorities to know where he was. These plans required that the location of the house should not be disclosed, not even to Peter, and involved a private agreement between Jesus and the owner of the house, not only for the loan of the room, but a procedure by which Jesus' emissaries would locate the building. Probably inside the city gate by the Pool of Siloam they would encounter the man with a pitcher of water, readily noticed since water was commonly fetched by women. They would not speak to the man, only follow where he led, and they would enter the house which the man entered. Jesus had given them specific words to say to the householder to prove that they had, in fact, come from Jesus. Obviously, the coming of these disciples was awaited, since when they identified themselves by reciting the correct formula, they were immediately shown the large upper room which was already prepared for the occasion. The instructions of Jesus convey that at some time he had privately visited the house and had seen the room, and that he had obtained the assent of the mysterious householder.

While the identity of the house owner is not our present concern, we may note that he is a man of substance. For the building to have a large upper room it could not have belonged to some poor workman. So much was this consequential citizen of Jerusalem in the confidence of Jesus, though clearly he was not one of the apostolic band, that Jesus can ask of him a dangerous favor and rely on him implicitly not to betray him.

The stratagem Jesus devises, and which is acted upon, is plainly designed to provide maximum security. We do not know when the arrangement was made, but it cannot have been at the last minute, for Jesus had left Jerusalem two days previously.

The movements of Jesus during Passion Week have to be observed. He knew that the authorities wanted to arrest him. Indeed, he openly and deliberately had goaded them into taking action by his behavior and speech in the temple, beginning with the wrecking of the temple market. What stymied the authorities was that Jesus was always surrounded by crowds of Jews who would have raised a tumult if there had been any attempt to seize him. At the inflammable season of the Passover, there was even the risk of an armed outbreak by the militants against the Romans in which multitudes would lose their lives.

Here, Jesus takes further precautions to obviate the possibility of arrest or, conceivably, assassination. He visits Jerusalem and the temple always in company and only in the daytime. He never spends a night in the city or remains within its walls after dark, except on Passover Eve itself, when, as we have seen, he has provided a means to keep his whereabouts secret. After the Last Supper, Jesus again leaves the city. Evidently, Judas Iscariot had been made aware that it was Jesus' intention to go to the Garden of Gethsemane, there to await arrest. It is clearly Jesus himself who dictates when, where, and how events affecting him are to happen.

Jesus has assured his safety on previous nights by making his headquarters at the home of trustworthy friends at the village of Bethany, east of Jerusalem on the far side of the Mount of Olives. Between Bethany and the city, the ground was covered with the tents of thousands of Jewish pilgrims who had gone to Jerusalem for the festival and could not find accommodation within the walls. In particular, there was a reception area allocated to pilgrims from Galilee. No police or soldiers could have penetrated this human barrier without word reaching Jesus, and the risk of riot was too great to make the attempt. Our investigation has to be guided in this respect, as in others, by all the information we can glean—religious, social, political, and topographical. The results furnish strong circumstantial evidence.

The episode of the Last Supper reveals Jesus in a light in which the Church never represents him: as a skilled strategist with a fertile imagination. He is a man whose mind is busy with schemes to attain his own ends and defeat the plots of his enemies. He exercises such a powerful influence on others that they are ready to do his bidding, and he is by no means averse to employing methods and devices characteristic of human ingenuity.

We also have a revelation in this incident of how little we really know about the activities of Jesus. Evidently, he has a private life to which the apostles had no access, and relations with individuals of consequence in whom he could confide and rely upon when the apostles could not be trusted or were incapable of being of service. He would have needed such persons for his purposes, especially in and around Jerusalem. There must be much more than what is told of the family at Bethany, of Nicodemus, of Joseph of Arimathaea, of the unnamed householder who lent his upper room.

In all honesty, no one can suggest that this assessment is an exaggeration in conflict with the evidence. Any evasion would simply reflect unwillingness to face the realities. Perhaps, if this incident stood alone, it might be represented that Mark has been somewhat imaginative in his description. As it is, however, we have another event so public in character that it must have been very widely known, in the course of which Jesus employed a device similar to the one he had used in obtaining the householder's room for the Passover meal. The occasion was the Messianic entry of Jesus into Jerusalem a few days before the Passover.

With his disciples and a multitude of Galilean pilgrims going up to the capital for the festival, Jesus had crossed the Jordan near Jericho, ascending towards Jerusalem from the east. Again we quote Mark's Gospel:

> And when they came nigh to Jerusalem, unto Bethphage and Bethany, at the mount of Olives, he sendeth forth two of his disciples, and saith unto them, "Go your way into the village over against you: and as soon as ye be entered into it, ye shall find a colt tied, whereon never man sat; loose him and bring him. And if any man say unto you, 'Why do ye this?' say ye that the Master hath need of him; and straightway he will send him hither."
>
> And they went their way, and found the colt tied by the door without in a place where two ways met; and they loose him. And certain of them that stood there said unto them, "What do ye, loosing the colt?" And they said unto them even

as Jesus had commanded, and they let them go. And they brought the colt to Jesus, and cast their garments on him; and he sat upon him.

And many spread their garments in the way: and others cut down branches off the trees, and strawed them in the way. And they that went before, and they that followed, cried, saying, "Hosanna; Blessed is he that cometh in the name of the Lord: blessed be the kingdom of our father David, that cometh in the name of the Lord: Hosanna in the highest" (Mark 11:1–10).

Comparison with the other Gospels makes it clear that it was Jesus' intention to ride into Jerusalem on the foal of an ass as a symbolic act proclaiming that he was the King Messiah, according to the prophesy of Zechariah cited by Matthew and John. We notice that Jesus does not issue his instructions until he is close to the city, so there is no question that he was only tired after the long uphill journey from Jericho. At any time he could have had the loan of a beast from someone in the pilgrim band. Those who accompany Jesus have no doubt of the significance of his action, as the burden of their joyful cries indicates.

The demand of Jesus for a donkey thus can be seen to have been carefully staged, and staged precisely at the village of Bethany where Jesus had intimate friends—the sisters Martha and Mary and their brother Lazarus—with whom he had become acquainted the previous autumn. The Gospel writers, full of their exalted and superhuman view of Jesus, fail to discern the significance of what they are reporting from tradition. But when we study their accounts objectively, we can see that the donkey was in the position where the two disciples (again two) found him, because Jesus had made this request in a prearranged design. As with the Last Supper dispositions, words of identification—"The Master needs him"—had been agreed upon long in advance to assure that the donkey, identifiable because it was to be tethered by the door of a house at a road junction at the entrance of the village, would only be released to the right persons.

It is surely clear that the Bethany family, like the householder in Jerusalem, had faithfully and without question honored a request Jesus had made of them in strict secrecy when he was with them on an earlier occasion, and which he had not divulged, even to his apostolic intimates.

The issues are of such vital consequence in elucidating the riddle of the empty tomb that we must reiterate what we have deduced about Jesus' tactics. Between the two incidents, we have cited a strong similarity in the methods employed, both revealing Jesus as a man of invention and resourcefulness, methodically putting into operation plans of his devising to procure his ends. These strategic plans called for the services of persons of standing in and around Jerusalem, persons who could be counted upon absolutely for their devotion and discretion. The plans were evidently of such a nature that the disciples of Jesus from Galilee, even the closest of them, could not be made privy to them, since they could not contribute to their success and well might endanger their realization. Their part was to obey orders as the schemes were progressively put into operation.

From the kind of devices we have demonstrated, a Jesus emerges who we may look at with a new realization and perhaps with a new understanding and different kind of appreciation. He is a man who can command personal devotion, so that those who are powerfully influenced by him are ready to do whatever he may demand without knowing more than he cares to tell them. He is also very much of a mystery man, keeping his own counsel and pursuing his own ends with iron resolve. He is one who is very clear about what he has to accomplish, and he has the brains and ingenuity to achieve it step by step. He also knows what he is up against, and has the wit to discern how he can circumvent the designs of his enemies. Such a man, and only such a man, could make the dispositions relating to himself which the climax of his life apparently demanded. To go to the cross and yet survive it were essentials demanding the most intricate planning and timing, as well as a very clear perspective. Here again there were those whose services would be vital to success, and, as we have deduced, they were available and were given their instructions. Prominent among them was Joseph of Arimathaea, whom we now begin to appreciate could not have been acting on his own initiative.

11
As It Is Written

The more we probe into what has been transmitted in the Gospels, especially regarding the last six months of Jesus' life, the clearer it becomes that he is not the victim of circumstances over which he has no control. On the contrary, his movements and actions are deliberate, carefully calculated, and intentional. The Gospel writers, though their information was very limited, are aware of this to an extent; but from their viewpoint there was no requirement to analyze and investigate. They were satisfied that everything that took place affecting Jesus had been predicted in the Old Testament Scriptures, and that Jesus was aware of these prophecies, or in any case was equipped with divine foreknowledge.

Nothing in the Scriptures, however, could be said to convey at what time and season, and in what manner and sequence, the predictions would be fulfilled. Consequently, Jesus had to have an extraordinary capacity to conceive a systematic progression of events in which he would figure as Messiah, and a remarkable strategy and willpower to bring about the required results.

The entire undertaking obtained its relevance and impetus only if it is assumed that Jesus had come to the conviction that he was the Messiah his people were awaiting. We have here, then, a man living at a time when a miraculous intervention on God's part was expected by the Jewish nation, a man with an intense and peculiar conviction which supplied the driving force to the fertile contrivances of his brain.

We have to establish the circumstances very clearly, because we are required to adjust ourselves to peculiar beliefs and modes of thought. These ideas are based on the premise that Jesus could and did determine his own fate, enlisting the help of persons upon whom he could depend to carry out the duties assigned to them. Since the climax was to be reached in Jerusalem, involving the government (Roman and Jewish), it was in and around the city that he needed the services of influential individuals. We have an indication of the identity of some of those who played a part in the chain of events. There was the family at Bethany, evidently people of some standing. There was Joseph of Arimathaea and Nicodemus, both members of the Jewish governing council. There was the Beloved Disciple of the Fourth Gospel, whom we have called John the Priest, a man with access to the high priest's palace and known to him personally, whom (see Chapter 4) we may not be wrong in identifying as the owner of the house in which the Last Supper was held. It would appear that all of these people were awaiting the Messiah and the establishment of the Kingdom of God in the world.

Abundant evidence exists both in Jewish and Christian records that the time in which Jesus lived had been pronounced by interpreters of the Bible to fall within those Last Times, or the End of the Days, in which the Messiah would appear and Israel would be saved. Consequently, the Jewish people were deeply stirred and eagerly awaiting miraculous developments, which should deliver them from their foes and herald the institution of a peaceful and just world order.

There was an outpouring of apocalyptic literature heralding the great Judgment and Deliverance, as well as the novel treatment of the canonical Scriptures as oracular. The Bible, and especially the Prophets, had contained many intimations of the future, near and remote, in a variety of contexts. But now, in circles like those of the Essenes, it was accepted that the whole of the Bible, and not merely sections of it, was of prophetic import relating essentially to the Last Times. The text, therefore, was to be understood by the enlightened and instructed not in the natural or literal sense, nor with sole relevance to ancient circumstances, but as foretelling what would come to pass in the experiences of the faithful in the End Time. Some of these interpretations are now in our possession in the recovered Dead Sea Scrolls. But there were different schools of thought, and the explanations varied accordingly.

That the Old Testament should be treated oracularly comes as no surprise to the Christian. He is accustomed from the New Testament to take for granted that all the significant incidents in the life of Jesus in his role as the Christ should have been predicted in the Jewish Bible. *So it was written.* Yet an examination of most of the passages cited, taking them in their original context, shows that they refer to other persons entirely and to a variety of different matters, and that their particular application to Jesus is forced and far-fetched. The early Christians, obviously, had their own school of interpretation in the manner of their contemporaries in Palestine, and thus could hold that the experiences of Jesus had been prophetically foretold.

As we can see from the writings of the early Church Fathers from the end of the first century, the Jewish Bible (particularly in the Greek version) was ransacked for passages that could be construed as prophetic of circumstances affecting Jesus, but also of those affecting the Church, especially in relation to the evangelization of the Gentiles and the rejection of the Jews as God's chosen people. We have only to read the so-called *Epistle of Barnabas* and the works of Justin Martyr in the second century for a better understanding of what happened.

This requisitioning of Old Testament "evidence" must go back to the very beginning of Christian activity. Without such "testimonies," the Jewish followers of Jesus would have found it virtually impossible to persuade many of their faith that he was the expected Messiah—especially if his crucifixion by the Romans was interpreted as his failure. Thus we find the apostle Paul at Thessalonica seeking out the synagogues of the Jews.

And Paul, as his manner was, went in unto them, and three sabbath days reasoned with them out of the scriptures, opening and alleging, that Christ must needs have suffered, and risen again from the dead; and that this Jesus, whom I preach unto you, is Christ" (Acts 17:2–3).

Although it is not claimed that the Christian apostles originally employed the Bible oracularly for Messianic purposes relating to Jesus, we do find them exploiting and extending it. According to them, they had acquired the technique from Jesus himself.

Jesus is represented as a master of Messianic lore. But, as we have said, his qualifications in this respect were regarded as part of his divine endowment. In John, when Jesus teaches in the temple, the Jews marvel, saying, "How knoweth this man learning, having never studied?" Jesus replies, "My doctrine is not mine, but his that sent me" (John 7:15–16). He also tells the Jews at another time that Moses had written about him (5:46).

We encounter several intimations of Jesus to his disciples, especially after he had acknowledged to them at Caesarea-Philippi that he was the Messiah, of what would befall him. And what he told them about his own fate, as well as that of his forerunner John the Baptist as the returned Elijah, ran very contrary to their own Messianic anticipations (Matthew 16:21, 17:10 – 13). We have to determine whether we are in contact with reliable tradition when we consider all the predictions Jesus is reported to have made of his sufferings, his death at the hands of the Jewish and Gentile authorities, and then his resurrection and ascension. Did his followers subsequently attribute these sayings to Jesus to demonstrate that his crucifixion did not prove he was not the Messiah? Quite the reverse is the case, since the Bible had foretold the circumstances of the Messiah's fate and Jesus had disclosed, in advance, knowledge of what was to come.

Of course, Jesus well may have said something about what was in store for him, and, for propaganda purposes, the Evangelists may have used the Church's instruction of these matters to make it more explicit. Even if he had not spoken freely about his destiny, Jesus could not have planned his experience in advance unless he believed that he was fulfilling a destiny laid down cryptically in the Bible.

But it would surely be wrong to credit Jesus with the belief that the Old Testament was an exact and explicit "book of fate" in which all the circumstances pertaining to the Messiah had been directly foretold. If Jewish expectation had followed these predictions precisely, there would have been no room for divergent opinions on almost everything relating to the messianic hope. Had there been exact prerequisites, there would have been one agreed exegesis on the subject to guide and test any would-be claimant of messiahship. Nothing of the kind was in existence. Even the Essenes had to get their results by devious and far-fetched methods peculiar to themselves, which gave opportunities to others to try their hand at prophetic interpretation, Jesus among them.

So much happened to Jesus, unexpected in popular imagination and contradictory of his messiahship, that it was imperative for the early Christians to have proof-texts at their command conveying that these very things had been predicted in detail.

When I put forward the view in *The Passover Plot* that Jesus had planned his fate from his own interpretation of what was demanded and Scripturally foreseen, many pious Christians were horrified. They readily accepted that all that happened to Jesus was a fulfillment of prophecy, but with Jesus as the predetermined victim. They objected to the thesis that Jesus had any hand in the events that took place or organized things intentionally to correspond to Old Testament predictions.

Scornfully these critics asked, how could Jesus have brought about so much that was wholly beyond his control, such as his betrayal for thirty pieces of silver, or the soldiers at the crucifixion casting lots for his clothing? Even more, what could Jesus have possibly done about the circumstances of his birth and infancy? Had not these events been prophesied?

My opponents were simply taking the unscholarly view that such incidents had been directly predicted in the Old Testament and took place because they were so predicted. In fact, the Old Testament passages cited had no connection, prophetic or otherwise, with the events to which they were applied. What I was doing was crediting Jesus with making certain inferences in the Essene manner to obtain guidance on the part the Messiah should play, not with a wholesale pinpointing of events in the manner represented in the Gospels and later Christian literature.

If we are to accept that Jesus planned his fate—and that he had a hand in the ordering of events we have already demonstrated—then we should try to discover whether he had particular sources that impressed and influenced him in devising the course he would pursue. It well may be, as the Gospels state, that Jesus did on occasion convey to his disciples that events were following a predicted course (compare Mark 9:11–13). But there is no suggestion that he did this continually and on any large scale prior to his death. Otherwise, the disciples would have been fully prepared for all that would transpire, including the resurrection. Evidently they were not, and this ignorance is admitted (as in John 20:8 – 9). Luke's Gospel makes it very clear that, after his resurrection, Jesus gave his followers comprehensive and specific instructions in applying prophetic biblical passages of what would befall him.

The first recipients of such enlightenment are two disciples who are overtaken by the risen Jesus on the road to Emmaus, though they do not recognize him. In response to his asking why they are so sad, they tell the stranger what had been their hopes of Jesus, how these wishes had been defeated by his unexpected death on the cross, and then how they had been puzzled by the reported disappearance of his body. The stranger then takes them to task:

> O fools, and slow of heart to believe all that the prophets have spoken: ought not Christ [i.e., the Messiah] to have suffered these things, and to enter into his glory? And beginning at Moses and all the Prophets, he expounded unto them in all the Scriptures the things concerning himself (Luke 24:25–27).

Later, apparently the next day, Jesus appears in his own form to the company of his disciples in Jerusalem, convincing them he is no ghost by eating some broiled fish and a piece of honeycomb. He tells them:

> *These are the words which I spake unto you, while I was yet with you, that all things must be fulfilled, which were written in the Law of Moses, and in the Prophets, and in the Psalms, concerning me. Then opened he their understanding, that they might understand the Scriptures, and said unto them, Thus it is written, and thus it behoved Christ to suffer, and to rise from the dead the third day: and that repentance and remission of sins should be preached in his name among all nations, beginning at Jerusalem. And ye are witnesses of these things (Luke 24:44–48).*

The first sentence suggests that Luke well may be quoting the opening words of a primitive Nazorean prophetic *Testimony Book*. It is of note that in the above passage Jesus refers to the Hebrew Bible in its three divisions: the Law (Torah), the Prophets, and the Psalms (as the first book of the Hagiographa).

But John's Gospel, the one we have termed the Resurrection Gospel, insists more than any of the others that all that is said to have happened had to happen because of the Bible predictions. Everything takes place inescapably, of necessity. Fulfillment is fated, inevitable, and cannot be varied one iota. Jesus knows this prophecy in advance and perforce must go along with it; but it often dawns on the disciples only after Jesus has left this world. Let us quote some of the particularly Johannine passages:

> *Jesus answered and said unto them [i.e., the Jews], Destroy this temple, and in three days I will raise it up. . . . But he spake of the temple of his body. When therefore he was risen from the dead, his disciples remembered that he had said this unto them; and they believed the scripture, and the word which Jesus had said (John 2:19 – 22; see also John 2:13 – 17).*

> *[Jesus says to the Jews] Search the Scriptures; for in them ye think ye have eternal life: and they are they which testify of me (John 5:39).*

> *Jesus stood and cried, saying . . . He that believeth on me,*

as the scripture hath said, out of his belly shall flow rivers of living water. But this spake he of the Spirit, which they that believe on him should receive: for the Holy Ghost was not yet given, because that Jesus was not yet glorified (John 7:37–39).

And Jesus, when he had found a young ass, sat thereon; as it is written, Fear not, daughter of Sion: behold thy king cometh, sitting on an ass's colt. These things understood not his disciples at the first: but when Jesus was glorified, then remembered they that these things were written of him, and that they had done these things unto him (John 12:14–16).

But though Jesus had done so many miracles before them [i.e., the Jews], yet they believed not on him: that the saving of Esaias the prophet might be fulfilled, which he spake, Lord, who hath believed our report? and to whom hath the arm of the Lord been revealed? Therefore they could not believe, because that Esaias said again, He hath blinded their eyes, and hardened their heart; that they should not see with their eyes, nor understand with their heart, and be converted, and I should heal them (John 12:37–40).

If ye know these things, happy are ye if ye do them. I speak not of you all: I know whom I have chosen: but that the scripture may be fulfilled, He that eateth bread with me hath lifted up his heel against me (John 13:17–18).

The Jews therefore said unto him [i.e., Pilate], It is not lawful for us to put any man to death: that the saying of Jesus might be fulfilled, which he spake, signifying what death he should die (John 18:31–32; see also John 12:32–33).

Then the soldiers, when they had crucified Jesus, took his garments ... and also his coat: now the coat was without seam, woven from the top throughout. They said therefore among themselves, Let us not rend it, but cast lots for it, whose it shall be: that the scripture might be fulfilled which saith, They parted my garments among them, and for my vesture they did cast lots. These things therefore the soldiers did (John 19:23–24).

*After this, Jesus knowing that all things were now ac-
complished, that the scriptures might be fulfilled, saith, I
thirst (John 19:28; reference to Psalm 69:21).*

*Then came the soldiers, and brake the legs of the first, and
of the other which was crucified with him. But when they
came to Jesus, and saw that he was dead already, they brake
not his legs: but one of the soldiers with a spear pierced his
side. . . . For these things were done that the scripture should
be fulfilled, A bone of him shall not be broken. And again
another scripture saith, They shall look on him whom they
pierced (John 19:32–37).*

*Then went in also that other disciple [i.e., into the sepul-
chre], . . . and he saw and believed. For as yet they knew not
the scripture, that he must rise again from the dead (John
20:8–9).*

Everything happens in John because it must, and every event
is found to fulfill a prophecy. It is only a question of discerning
by the Spirit the relevant Old Testament text. But Jesus, having
the Spirit, knows in advance everything that has to take place,
and, what is more, deliberately says or does certain things
because a Biblical passage, rightly interpreted, calls for them.

The position taken by the early Church is understandable,
because if Jesus was not the Messiah (the Christ), and even more
the divine Son of God, then Christianity was without justification. The Church could not be satisfied with being just another
mystery religion with a mythological basis. The contention was
that all the circumstances related to Jesus had happened historically, in real life, and had been anticipated and certified in detail
by ancient authoritative holy books.

But the Christians were looking back, searching the Scriptures
with hindsight, while Jesus was compelled to look forward.
There was nothing set down in an orderly arrangement, covering the most minute particulars, that could guide his steps
along a prescribed Messianic path. There were certain intimations and interpretations, diverse and unorganized, from which

there had to be constructed, at the discretion and by the ingenuity of individuals and groups, some kind of outline of Messianic matters.

We hold that Jesus did indeed believe in prophecy, and drew ingredients from the Bible that enabled him to build a pattern of what was incumbent upon the Messiah. These ingredients spoke to him of suffering and subsequent triumph in the task of redeeming Israel and, through Israel, the world. We shall seek to enter into his thinking. But we find no justification for treating him as an automaton, devoid of independent initiative.

12
The Sure Mercies
of David

The Christian Church, with its quasi-pagan background, could readily envisage a divine Son of God who came into the world with the express object of sacrificing himself to expiate human sin, so that those who believed in him should be freed from guilt and entitled to a blissful immortality. But such a Son of God, while experiencing the death of the physical body he had assumed, could not be defeated by it: he—the immortal—had to return to the heaven whence he came. Moreover, in so doing, he had to certify that death for man had been vanquished by taking the renewed flesh of his manhood back to heaven with him. It was here that the Jewish doctrine of human resurrection rendered a valuable service. It was pounced on by the Dear Disciple, not only as an explanation of the empty tomb but as the inevitable sequel to the proposition of incarnation and sacrifice.

The faith of the Jewish followers of Jesus did not envisage any divine incarnation, yet it was greatly in need of conviction of a resurrection. A dead Jesus, who remained dead, could not be the Messiah. But resurrection, followed by ascension, was just

the solution needed to explain the puzzling and tragic circumstances. Here was no divine being returned to his place of
origin where as God he truly belonged; but a Messiah being
rewarded for his faithfulness by being welcomed On High for a
brief period was another matter. There was precedent, as in the
case of Elijah, for one being taken to heaven in order to return.
Enoch had been translated, and assumption was being claimed
for Moses in Essenite circles. The Bible also spoke of a Son of
Man borne on clouds into the presence of God to receive a
kingdom that would endure forever (Daniel 7:13–14); and was it
not said by God of the king in the Psalms (110), "Sit thou at my
right hand, *until* I make thine enemies thy footstool"?

From the Messianic viewpoint we can see that without Christian intervention, there was no call for the Messiah to die before
he inaugurated his earthly kingdom. Even in John's Gospel, it is
agreed that after Jesus implied in an ambiguous saying, what
kind of death he should die, he was answered by the people,
"We have heard out of the Law that Christ [i.e., the Messiah]
abideth for ever: and how sayest thou, the Son of Man must be
lifted up?" (John 12:32–34). The Jewish view equally comes out
in Luke, on no less authority than the angel Gabriel, who tells
the prospective mother of Jesus: "The Lord shall give unto him
the throne of his father David: and he shall reign over the house
of Jacob for ever; and of his kingdom there shall be no end"
(Luke 1:32–33).

The prophetic image of the ideal king to come of David's line
assumes that his reign would not be interrupted by death, thus
necessitating a resurrection. And it is now widely recognized by
scholars in the Christian church that Isaiah 53 is not a prediction of the Messiah's death. That the Messiah should suffer was
not an alien concept, but it did not follow that death would be
the consequence. It is therefore proper to ask, did Jesus expect
to die?

To answer such a question, a very vital question, we must
attempt to penetrate into Jesus' Messianic thinking. We cannot
expect too much from the Gospels in this respect, since their
authors lived and wrote after the capture of Jerusalem by the
Romans in 70 A.D., a period when the Christian message was
becoming increasingly adapted to gentile concepts. But since

these authors did reflect earlier Christian beliefs and documentation to an extent, some indications were bound to remain of how Jesus saw and set about his Messianic task.

A precious evidence and vital clue is to be found in the preservation of the testimony that Jesus was descended from King David and thus was entitled to claim that he was the Davidic Messiah. Dangerous as it was to affirm this within the Roman Empire, especially in the decades following the Jewish revolt against the Romans, the truth was not discarded. The relations of Jesus, including a first cousin and two great nephews, were the objects of an imperial attempt to round up the surviving members of the house of David. The one or two Gospel statements, almost entirely confined to Mark and John, which seek to subordinate the royalty of Jesus to his divinity, only serve to illustrate the inescapable fact that he was a descendant of David, a fact significant for himself as well as for his Jewish followers.

The evidence of his lineage is one we have to accept as primitive, since it goes back to a document—Paul's letter to the believers at Rome—written well before the Jewish revolt, and only about twenty years after Jesus' death. Physically, declares Paul, Jesus was of the seed of David, but, he adds, that spiritually he also was demonstrated to be the Son of God by the most potent manner of his resurrection from the dead (Romans 1:3 — 4).

The Messianic Hope derived its chief justification and impetus from the often repeated Biblical affirmation of God's perpetual covenant with David (compare Psalms 89:20 — 29; Jeremiah 33:17–21), which guaranteed that the ultimate ideal king who would reign forever would be of Davidic descent (Isaiah 11). Indeed, the Prophet Ezekiel sees an incarnation of David as the prince of the Messianic Age (Ezekiel 34:23; 37:24).

From age to age, Jewish popular sentiment clung to the memory of the shepherd boy, the man after God's heart, who became a king (1 Samuel 13:14; Acts 13:22–23).

He chose David also his servant, and took him from the sheepfolds: from following the ewes great with young he brought him to feed Jacob his people, and Israel his inheri-

tance. So he fed them according to the integrity of his heart;
and guided them by the skillfulness of his hands (Psalms
78:70–72).

Certainly to those who first recorded the climax of Jesus' life,
the thought of him as Son of David was very strongly present,
and the Book of Psalms was found to be the best interpreter as
well as anticipator of what transpired.

What, then, of Jesus himself? Knowing from childhood of his
family's royal descent, must he not have loved the account of his
famous ancestor's adventures as related in the books of the
Prophet Samuel, and have sung with fervor and appreciation the
songs attributed to him? One of the Hebrew prayers of his time
which he would have recited regularly called on God, "Speedily
cause the branch of David, thy servant, to sprout, and let his
horn be exalted by thy salvation; because daily do we wait for
thy salvation" (*Amidah*).

We do not know positively what influences, parental and
other, conveyed to the mind of the young Jesus the possibility
that he might be destined to be the Messiah. But it would be
very surprising if he had entertained no notion of such a pros-
pect before he went to the Jordan to encounter John the Baptist
and then embark upon his public activities. The sureness with
which he sets about his task argues a long-standing conviction
of status and purpose; this in turn argues a prolonged prepar-
atory quest on his part for guidance and illumination of the
Messianic role. There were current views and interpretations
Jesus could have consulted for clarification in what have been
called his Silent Years before he reached the age of thirty. It
cannot be supposed as merely speculative that the life and
words of David were a formative source dear to him.

We have noted in the previous chapter that the early Church
attributed to Jesus the division of the Messiah's experiences into
two phases: "Ought not Christ to have suffered these things, and
to enter into his glory?" There developed the doctrine of the Two
Advents, one in humiliation and one in glory. Jewish thought
later developed the concept of a martyr Messiah who would
suffer and be followed by the Messiah of the House of David who

would reign. The interpreters of the Scriptures could point to the two phases in the life of the Patriarch Joseph, who first was enslaved and imprisoned and later became viceroy of Egypt and savior of his brethren. Moses also had to flee from Egypt as a fugitive, and return many years later to deliver his people from bondage.

But of those heroes whose experiences could serve as pointers to what should befall the Messiah, of particular interest to Jesus would be the adventures of David. His story also fell clearly into two phases. There was first the story of the shepherd boy, chosen by God to be king of Israel and anointed by the Prophet Samuel, but whose life was endangered by the reigning monarch, Saul, so that he was forced to lead the precarious existence of a hunted outlaw. Some of the Psalms spoke eloquently of his trials and tribulations, as well as how God saved him from death at the hands of his enemies. Then the promise was fulfilled that David would reign over all Israel and he was assured that his line would endure forever. To love and serve God, who promised to be a father to him, was his desire.

The words of the prophets, especially Isaiah, seem to have supported these records, since they spoke of a Suffering Servant of God who becomes God's chosen means of redeeming Israel and all nations. It was not far-fetched to deduce that the Messiah's destiny would call for an initial activity involving suffering and persecution, which, if endured with faithfulness, would be rewarded with world rulership when the Kingdom of God would be established on earth.

The idea that the Messiah might be called upon to give his life was not a natural inference from the intimations of the past, and there is no reason to suppose that Jesus would have entertained it. Consequently, a resurrection of the Messiah would not have presented itself as a necessity, as it did to the early Church.

In contemplating a course the Messiah should pursue, we would expect that Jesus would have taken his cue from the Psalms in particular. Was it not written:

> *Incline your ear, and come unto me: hear, and your soul shall live; and I will make an everlasting covenant with you,*

even the sure mercies of David. *Behold, I have given him for a witness to the people, a leader and commander to the people (Isaiah 55:3–4; compare Acts 13:32–37)?*

What were these "sure mercies of David" in the matter of life or death? In the Essene fashion, let us make a *catena* (chain) by stringing together without a break various passages from the Psalms, in the manner I employed in my books *The Passover Plot* and *For Christ's Sake.*

> *I shall not die, but live, and declare the works of the Lord. The Lord hath chastened me sore: but he hath not given me over unto death. Though I walk in the midst of trouble, thou wilt revive me: thou shalt stretch forth thine hand against the wrath of mine enemies, and thy right hand shall save me. Thou, which has shewed me great and sore troubles, shalt quicken me again, and shalt bring me up again from the depths of the earth. The bands of the grave compassed me about; the snares of death prevented me. In my distress I called upon the Lord, and cried unto my God: he heard my voice, out of his temple, and my cry came before him, even into his ears. Then the earth shook and trembled; the foundations of the hills moved and were shaken. . . . He sent from above, he took me, he drew me out of great waters. He delivered me from my strong enemy. I have set the Lord always before me: because he is at my right hand, I shall not be moved. Therefore my heart is glad, and my glory rejoiceth: my flesh also shall rest in hope. For thou wilt not leave my soul in the grave; neither wilt thou suffer thy holy one to see corruption. Thou wilt show me the path of life; in thy presence is fullness of joy: at thy right hand are pleasures for evermore. God will redeem my soul from the grasp of the grave: for he shall receive me. The king shall joy in thy strength, O Lord; and in thy salvation how greatly shall he rejoice! . . . Thou settest a crown of pure gold on his head. He asked life of thee, and thou gavest it him, even length of days for ever and ever. His glory is great in thy salvation; honor and majesty hast thou laid upon him.*

The sequence of quotations is as follows: Psalms 118:17–18; 138:7;

71:20; 18:5 — 7, 16 — 17; 16:8 — 11;49:15; 21:1 — 5. These passages were chosen because they are concerned with the theme of suffering and salvation. Even Psalm 22, in which the early Church saw reference to the circumstances of Jesus' crucifixion, claims that God heard and responded to the sufferer's cry for deliverance from the fate determined by his enemies.

Surely what a sentient Son of David could glean from these graphic poetic passages would be that while the Messiah might be called upon to endure great torment at the hands of his opponents—enough that he would go down into the very jaws of death—his life would be preserved whole in him. Deliverance would be granted and a means of escape would be revealed to him. We have here the language of a man whose life is sought, hunted down, and exhausted, finding concealment in a cavern as in a tomb, yet a man who is confident that he will survive to fulfill his destiny because it is God's will. In the time of Jesus, the new techniques of oracular interpretation would have been able to discover a relevance of the words to much later circumstances, and they would have spoken in particular as a revelation from the past, from David to David's greater son.

Because of what has been conceived as the atoning virtue of Jesus' death, it has not been recognized that Jesus himself may have put an entirely different interpretation on the scriptural images. Had that been the case, he would have known that death was not required of him, and he would have received illumination on how to cheat death of his prey. So had it been with Abraham and his son Isaac. Their wills and love of God had been tested, but the death of Isaac had not been demanded. Similarly, the Messiah would be shown a way, if he was faithful. He would indeed return from the tomb, but with no need of resurrection, since life would never have departed from his body. Accordingly, I have argued that Jesus laid his plans on this basis, which would cheat only his foes of the results of their evil designs.

In Psalms 2, the rulers take counsel against the Lord and his anointed; but God laughs at their folly, and despite them will set His king upon the holy hill of Zion.

To follow prophetic guidance, Jesus could not evade suffering. Clearly, had he been so minded, Jesus could have stayed away from Jerusalem, and never allowed himself to be acclaimed

Messiah, king of the Jews. But in so doing, he committed an act of high treason against Caesar that assured that he would be arrested and crucified. Although he knew full well what the experience of crucifixion involved in physical torment, he courted it deliberately. His decision could only have been prompted out of a deep sense of conviction that such a course was essential to shock his people into committing their cause to God and turning back to Him in faith and repentance. To carry out this fate called for tremendous courage and an iron resolve, which he could manifest because of his own confidence in his mission and destiny.

Thus we are stating nothing detrimental to the character and dignity of Jesus, nor anything contrary to what the Gospels convey of him as a man, when we proposed that, with single-ness of mind and the sure touch of a master, he set a course and laid plans to achieve his objectives. God willing, that course and these plans would lead through the valley of the shadow of death to a reward of victory and triumph. Such a man thus could lift up the cup of blessing at the Passover Supper with a steady hand and announce: "This signifies my blood of the new covenant, which is shed for many. Verily I say unto you, I will drink no more of the fruit of the vine, until that day that I drink it new in the Kingdom of God" (Matthew 26:28 — 29).

13
A Man Alone

Behind the riddle of the empty tomb, we have deduced the operation of a plan of action so bizarre that only a very singular man could have contrived it. The man who fits the requirements is the one to whom the plan relates, and who is its instigator and at the center of all the circumstances. It is to Jesus himself that we must look for enlightenment both on the motivation and the realization of the details. We have already seen him as a man with a strong sense of destiny and a very alert mind, a man who was both a brilliant organizer and strategist. What more can we learn about him that will help clear up the mystery we are seeking to unravel?

The Gospels disclose a number of Jesus' personality traits, among them, that he was very sensitive and emotional. He wept in public, lamenting over Jerusalem and at the tomb of Lazarus, and no doubt on other occasions. He was prone to outbursts of anger, denouncing his opponents in scathing terms. On the other hand, he evidently took to individuals with a ready affection. He was full of compassion, concerned with children, the sick and the elderly, the poor and needy. In the midst of a milling crowd, when someone deliberately touched him, he was instantly aware of it. He pitied the outcast and associated freely and happily with the dregs of society, obtaining a reputation among the respectable for being a glutton and drunkard.

But though he was evidently gregarious and enjoyed being with people, he was not really an extrovert. He gave an impression of paternalism, of moving about with regal benevolence of being a king among his subjects. This was not a pose, but the effect of the secret of his Messianic identity, which he carried about with him and did not disclose until near the climax of his activities. He referred often to the secrets of the Kingdom of God.

The task of Jesus as Messiah was to influence others—more especially, "the lost sheep of the house of Israel." Repentance was the passport to deliverance. His business, therefore, was with the masses, whose condition under oppression had largely destroyed faith and morality and had fostered a spirit of violence and retaliation. He had to woo them back to the ways of God.

Yet behind this tremendous effort was an ever-watchful and lonely man, needing continually to have his spirit refreshed and his powers restored by prayer and meditation. There was an inborn solitariness in his nature, which increased with the growing claims upon his mind of the destiny he believed to be his and what would be demanded of him to fulfill it. After his father's death there was no one in the world with whom he could share his problems and in whom he could confide. He was a man alone, committed to the most exacting undertaking and requiring what privacy was possible to ponder and to plan. This, at least to an extent, may explain why he did not take a wife.

This assessment arises partly from a consideration of what it must have meant to the young Jesus to entertain the notion that he might be the desperately awaited Deliverer, and partly from what is reflected in the Gospel reminiscences about him.

The man of mystery first comes before us as a boy in Luke's Gospel. At the age of twelve he travels to Jerusalem for the feast of Passover with his parents in a company of pilgrims from Galilee. On the return journey it is discovered that he is missing. Alarmed, his father and mother return to the city seeking him, and finally discover him in the temple among the doctors of the law, listening to them and asking questions. Berated by his relieved mother, Jesus expresses surprise that his parents should have been concerned about him and not have realized where he would be. Here the boy is anxious to obtain reliable information about things which are important to him, and clearly is quite unaware that a gap has opened between himself and his family so that they are not going along with him in the direction his mind is taking.

A much more decisive moment is when the Spirit comes upon him during his baptism, thus making him ready to embark on his Messianic enterprise. The Spirit drives him immediately into the wilderness to wrestle alone with Satan for the symbolic forty days. He rejects decisively that he should act in any other way than according to the will of God. There could be no evasions of responsibility, no short cuts to his goal.

Soon Jesus has his first experience with the grim determination of a crowd of the needy to gain its ends, in this case, physical healing. "And in the morning, rising up a great while before day, he went out, and departed into a solitary place, and there prayed" (Mark 1:32–35).

We have several Gospel references to Jesus' practice of seeking solitude away from the crowds, and even his disciples, for prayer and meditation. He found it necessary to be alone periodically to restore his strength and clarify his course of action, and he strongly disliked anyone witnessing his communing with his spirit and with his Maker. He denounced as hypocrites those who made a public parade of piety. "But thou, when thou prayest, enter into thy closet, and when thou hast shut thy door, pray to thy Father which is in secret; and thy Father which seeth in secret shall reward thee openly" (Matthew 6:5–6).

Jesus was evidently a very sensitive individual, and though not a loner he could only cope with the demands of his task by isolating himself from his surroundings. Even on the road, he would often walk alone, apparently oblivious to his disciples chattering behind him. Yet he was aware of what they were saying, and sometimes to their surprise broke in upon their talk with a pertinent remark.

But we also have to be conscious of a communications barrier which arose from Jesus' messianic convictions. Of necessity, at the outset of his public activities, he could not openly claim to be the Messiah or even admit it privately to his disciples (though John's Gospel conveys the contrary). Had he declared himself king of the Jews, or allowed others to hail him as such, he would have invited arrest and execution for high treason against Caesar. His mission would have ended when it had hardly begun. What would have happened can be ascertained by what followed almost immediately when Jesus publicly presented himself as Messiah during his triumphal entry into Jerusalem.

At the outset, Jesus had to operate in disguise under the ambiguous designation Son of Man (i.e., The Man), which in Jewish eclectic circles had certain messianic implications. In his occupation of preaching repentance in view of the speedy advent of the Kingdom of God, he presented himself much more as a religious than a political figure. This was not a mask, since Jesus believed his immediate mission was to seek and save the lost sheep among his people. On the dangerous topic of the Kingdom of God, Jesus expressed himself largely in parables, which contained nothing that a spy or informer could seize upon as seditious.

From the outset, therefore, there existed no possibility that Jesus could identify himself to his disciples: it would be much too risky. Neither could he discuss his plans and intentions with them. Because his intelligence excelled theirs, communication was further impeded. Jesus had to keep his own counsel in matters of utmost consequence. And towards the end, Jesus sought by interrogation to elicit his apostles' view of what they believed him to be. When Peter blurted out his conviction that Jesus was the Messiah, Jesus was extremely pleased that he had reached this conclusion, for which divine inspiration must have been responsible. Nevertheless, since the final hour had not yet come, Jesus insisted that the disciples should not disclose his identity to anyone.

Although the actions of Jesus were not clear to his followers, they were always purposeful; his references that his final hour had not yet come, or was imminent, give evidence of much advance secret planning and preparation. When the right moment did come, and not until then, Jesus "set his face steadfastly to go towards Jerusalem." If we compare Luke with John, this journey took place in the autumn prior to the spring of the following year when Jesus went to Jerusalem for the very last time. According to John's Gospel, the stay of Jesus on the former occasion lasted for some three months until about the end of December. Evidently there were very many things he had to do in the south, arrangements he had to make, for which the Galilean apostles, even those in his inner circle of disciples, would be of no service. Such arrangements, as we saw in Chapter 10, must have included those with the family at Bethany having a donkey tethered at an agreed upon spot, as well as those with the owner of the house with the large upper room, which included the rendezvous and signals that would enable the disciples to find the house without giving away its location in advance.

There were other vital arrangements to be made with various key individuals that required Jesus to travel periodically during this three-month stay in the south, in the vicinity of the capital. These departures apparently did not cause comment among the disciples, since he had done the same kind of thing on several occasions in Galilee. But to keep so much hidden from those around him must have imposed a very great strain on him, and the disciples were under stress too. As Galileans they were in alien and uncongenial surroundings, laughed at as uncouth with their country ways and barbarous dialect. Tension was building. Jesus had previously disclosed to them that he was the Messiah, and yet he was keeping them completely in the dark, communicating nothing to them of his designs. To their way of thinking, the impending events demanded preparations for an uprising and an assault on the Roman garrison, and contact with Zealot and disaffected elements, unless, that is, there was to be some stupendous miracle! Bickering developed on issues of precedence in the coming Kingdom and on the magnitude of rewards. They did not dare ask Jesus what they were supposed to do, stuck at Jerusalem for so long. They were becoming increasingly aware that they were under close observation by agents of a Jewish Council responsible for security to the Roman government, which itself was becoming increasingly restive about the intentions of the popular Galilean prophet.

Jesus could afford to give nothing away, no inkling of what

was going forward step by step. Discretion demanded that no one—not even the most responsible of those whose essential services were enlisted—should be fully knowledgeable about what Jesus was planning. Each would make only his own contribution, and for the most part would not know who else was participating or in what respect. Not only was this safer and better calculated to achieve success, but it minimized the personal risk for all those doing the bidding of Jesus. Their involvement was not to reason why. "The Master wishes this" had to suffice.

In the ensuing events, Jesus not only was pulling the strings and employing his knowledge, initiative, fertile imagination, and, yes, his faith in God, in the interests of the messianic redemption of his nation; he also was concentrating upon himself the suffering that would be a prelude to victory. Thus, the scriptures would be fulfilled.

14
The Riddle Read

We now conclude our investigation by attempting to reconstruct the circumstances that led up to and embraced the discovery that the tomb in which the body of Jesus was laid was empty less than two days after his crucifixion. The incidents relating to the tomb are revealed as falling within the framework of a comprehensive, well-planned operation, representing almost its last stage. When we look at what happened as part of the main features of Passion Week, we are able to perceive the accomplishments of a design that was premeditated and set in motion by Jesus himself.

Allowing for the differences in the Gospels and recognizing that they offer different, propagandistic aspects of the Christian interpretation, we have sufficient evidence to make a strong case for a unity of purpose that embraced a series of apparently distinct and diverse events surrounding the crucifixion. Events occurred fortuitously, as it might seem, and in obedience to prophetic requirements, leading to Jesus' resurrection and ascension. But the circumstances, when submitted to rational analysis, become much more eloquent in the context of a prearranged plan to accomplish a desired result. The key to the puzzle is the matter of motivation.

Without the empty tomb with its open entrance, no alternative propositions could have been conceived. It could be argued that the stone was moved by a supernatural agency so that a risen Jesus could make his exit. Alternatively, human hands could have been at work to remove Jesus as quickly as possible to give him medical treatment. No one had troubled to close the tomb again, possibly for reasons of haste or because it didn't matter since the tomb was now unoccupied. In any case, it was dangerous for the rescuers to delay their departure. They would have been arrested and probably executed had they been caught with the body.

What motive could Jesus have had for devising and putting into operation such an elaborate design as we have proposed? The Christian position holds that Jesus was born into our world as an incarnation of the divine Son of God with the express intention of sacrificing his life for human sin, so that all who believed in him would be forgiven by God and be granted the reward of blissful everlasting life. Death was the consequence of sin, and therefore to demonstrate that sin had been overcome, Jesus had to triumph over death and return to his Father in heaven to receive the reward of his faithfulness. What befell Jesus on earth was not the result of a sudden impulse on God's part, but the fulfillment of ancient prophetic intimations going back to the dawn of time. From this viewpoint, Jesus did not so much instigate what took place—although to an extent he did—as accept it to carry out God's will. For Jesus to be the comprehensive innovator of a very difficult plan was therefore uncalled for. In this case, it has to be complained that all the actors in the drama, though they might believe they were exercising free-will in what they did, were no more than human puppets. Where was the virtue in what Jesus did if there was no risk of absolute defeat and disaster?

It certainly can be argued that the suffering of Jesus, physically and emotionally, was genuine enough. That would be true whether he planned or did not plan his fate. But, with the Christian concept, the cry from the cross, "My God, my God, why hast thou forsaken me?", would lose much of its poignancy. It would seem to relate only to bodily pain and not to a genuine moment of despair, since the happy ending was never in doubt.

Theologians have sought to build up the agony of Jesus by arguing that in this moment of crisis he was carrying upon himself the whole fantastic weight of human sin, and thus God could stay with him no longer, as nothing evil could have access to His pure Presence.

The Christian reading of the story consequently calls for a highly sophisticated and extremely complex theological doctrine, an orchestration of events that is automatic in all its diverse elements, and it demands, as an essential part, appropriate divine intervention of a miraculous character.

Modern Church thinking is inclined to modify former positions. It accepts more positively that on earth the Son of God was wholly man; therefore, while Jesus had some understanding of what he was meant to accomplish, he was not completely sure how things would work out. He acted according to what he thought was God's will, to be rewarded and honored by God for his servant's fidelity.

This interpretation comes much closer to our understanding of Jesus' motives, which replaces certainty by personal convictions that were founded upon a prophetic reading of the Scriptures as they applied to the task and destiny of the Messiah. In this view, certain events might not have been accomplished as planned, or have taken an unexpected turn, regardless of how Jesus might have believed that what was written would be fulfilled.

Christian dogma has made it impossible to comprehend Jesus, since the conjunction of true God with true man defies analysis. Since Jewish expectation of the Messiah never conceived of him as superhuman or as an object of worship and adoration, we have to exclude wholly any idea of deity from the Messianic consciousness of Jesus. The Roman emperor might be God and man, and have his temples and priests, but not the king of the Jews. We therefore have to come down emphatically on the side of the total humanity of Christ, and in that light seek to grasp his aims as a Jew who came to believe he was the Messiah his people were so eagerly awaiting, and who sought to prime himself with knowledge of what was required of him in that capacity. It was he himself who had to order events aright to bring his task to fruition, and who therefore depended on divine guidance to instruct him. There was always the possibility that he was interpreting the believed predictions of the Scriptures wrongly, and thus was taking heroic risks that might have tragic consequences.

Jesus accepted the Essene position that his time was the climax of the Ages and the hardest time for Israel, since Satan now was using all his powers to lead God's people astray to prevent the coming of the Kingdom of God on earth. Satan (Belial) was the ruler of this world (compare Luke 4:5–6); the heathen kings and corrupt Jewish hierarchy were his minions. They were bound to be in league against the Lord's anointed (Psalms 2) to try to prevent the downfall of their master (Satan) when the kingdoms of this world would come under the government of God and of his Christ (Revelations 11:15). The initial function of the Messiah, therefore, was to rescue his people from the dominion of the Evil One by calling them to repentance and casting out demons, so that redeemed Israel might become the saviour of the gentiles ("salvation is of the Jews," John 4:22).

Despite Jesus' strenuous and exhausting efforts, neither words nor works availed on any scale to recover the lost sheep. A daring and salutary deed was called for. As their king, Jesus must shock his subjects into repentance as their proclaimed rightful monarch by a voluntary suffering on their behalf at the hands of the enemy. Such an event had to occur at the historically and psychologically appropriate moment of the Passover season, the season of Israel's liberation. All the resources of Jesus' fertile mind had to be enlisted in a daring and comprehensive plan, brilliantly conceived and executed in faith. The motivation is thus quite clear, and suggestions of fraud or deception are an absurdity. But comprehension of his mission depended on relating his purposes solely to the messianic vision of the holy men of his day. This vision was both unfamiliar and unacceptable to the non-Jewish world. It was so in the multinational Roman Empire at the beginning, and it is so equally in present-day society. This is the reason why so little of the real Jesus appears in the multiplicity of presentations about him. He is simply not wanted as he actually was.

However, let us at least make an effort to follow the workings of his mind. Then we shall perceive his high courage in deliberately putting himself in the power of the enemy, which was the power of the Evil One, in order as Messiah finally to break the chains of that power. The courage of Jesus was profound, because, although he had faith, he could not know positively whether he would succeed, since he had to rely on others to play their parts and was not acting alone. Moreover, he had to judge the reactions of his foes correctly.

What must be done had to be done at Jerusalem. The initiation of the plan, therefore, begins with the journey of Jesus to the capital at the season of the autumn festival of Tabernacles. There is marked here a division that cuts right across the ministry of the previous period. It is signified by the denunciation of the cities in which he had preached because they failed to repent; by the admission of Jesus to his disciples that he was the Messiah, coupled with the admonition not to reveal this to anyone; and by the execution of John the Baptist. By this time, it had become clear that the appeal to repentance because of the imminence of the Kingdom of God had failed. The message entrusted to the Twelve Apostles had fallen largely on deaf ears.

The purpose of Jesus at Jerusalem is—or certainly should be—transparently clear. He was not, as the gentile church imagined, now rejecting the Jews because they had rejected him. Jesus had been following in the steps of John the Baptist, and what had been rejected by the sinners in Israel was the call to repent and turn back to God. The Jewish populace could not be rejecting Jesus as their Messiah, since he had not openly claimed to be the Messiah. Quite to the contrary, he had rebuked those who hailed him as the Son of David.

The aim of Jesus now was in no way changed, but the means to bring it about was drastically altered. He planned to reveal himself as Messiah at the chosen moment in circumstances that would speak to the heart of his people louder than any words. But, first, much had to be worked out and appropriate preparations had to be made.

In the south, in the proximity of Jerusalem, Jesus was close to the center of Jewish worship and government. This location was essential in making his dispositions. While he had knowledge of the capital, he needed to study it more intimately—the situation of its principal buildings and the character of its different quarters, the plan of the Temple area, the details of its services, the manner in which Jewish affairs were conducted, and the movements of the Roman garrison. Every piece of information was valuable and could have a bearing on the decisions to be taken. Certain reactions had to be tested by attending the discussions of Jewish teachers held in the Temple cloisters in the court of the gentiles.

It was vital also to have friends at court, on the inside of government, in the entourage of the High Priest, and among members of the Jewish Council, the Sanhedrin, so that timely knowledge would reach Jesus of attitudes and intentions affecting him. In priestly circles Jesus already had John, the former follower of John the Baptist, who had a house probably in the priestly quarter on the Ophel close to the Temple. He also was acquainted with the councillor Nicodemus, and perhaps through him got to know another councillor, Joseph of Arimathaea. Both these men were awaiting the Kingdom of God. It is by no means unlikely that in the opposite direction, down towards the Dead Sea, Jesus would have had private conferences with the Essenes at Qumran.

It would not have been wise for Jesus to make his headquarters in Jerusalem, where he would be risking secret arrest before the time of his choice. Also, there was less possibility of being spied upon if he was living in the countryside within easy walking distance of the city. The little village of Bethany beyond the Mount of Olives offered him a suitable base with a well-to-do family devoted to him. From there, traveling to Jerusalem constantly down the Kidron Valley to the city gate near the Pool of Siloam, he discovered the pleasant and quiet retreat of the Garden of Gethsemane. Within the city, huddled at the foot of a valley between two hills, were the poor of Israel who awaited the Deliverer. The road from here led up through the Street of the Cheesemakers to the Temple, passing on the right the eminence of the ancient City of David. The designs of Jesus were to take account of these topographical features.

The plans formulated and organized between October and January were to be put into effect at the Passover in the ensuing spring. To accomplish his purpose, Jesus had to present himself to the multitudes assembled for the festival as the Messiah, the

Son of David, so there could be no question of the capacity in
which he was acting. It had to be clear that he would be
suffering for them as king of the Jews. How this was contrived is
on record in the account of the Triumphal Entry. The disclosure
of his identity also would assure, if communicated by the chief
priests to the Romans, that he would be arrested and brought
before the governor Pontius Pilate for judgment and crucifixion,
since claiming to be king of the Jews was an act of high treason
against Caesar. Because Jesus was so patently non-militant, the
chief priests would be reluctant to move unless provoked, since
a seizure of Jesus might precipitate a public outbreak of violence, causing many deaths, unless it could be done secretly
away from the Jewish masses. The wealthy hierarchy, therefore,
had to be goaded by fears that threatened their position, and
their animus aroused. To assure this objective, the Council's
fears of the aims of Jesus, already played upon, would be
brought to a retaliatory climax by his singular attack on the
temple market following his triumphal entry.

Jesus contrived the strategy so that the choice of time, place,
and circumstances of his arrest was his. We have already related
what he had prearranged with the owner of the house with the
large upper room so he would be able to celebrate the Passover
in Jerusalem unmolested. We do not know the manner in which
Jesus assured his betrayal by Judas Iscariot, one of the Twelve;
but the Gospels inform us that he did not doubt who his
betrayer was to be, and he would learn through his contacts in
the Sanhedrin and with the chief priests that an agreement with
Judas had been reached.

The most difficult and dangerous part of what Jesus planned
would come after he was arrested. From that moment he would
be almost entirely dependent on others to carry out their assigned tasks and would not be free to make any adjustments if
anything went wrong. This subjection was the great test of his
faith. He had chosen for Israel's sake that he would suffer on the
cross, and there must be no attempted rescue that might involve
the death of innocent people. This concern of his was evident at
Gethsemane, when he demanded that his arrest should not be
resisted or anyone captured but himself.

But Jesus read the scriptures, and notably the Psalms of

David, in the sense that, although tormented by his enemies, he would escape death, having demonstrated his faithfulness to the will of God. How could this escape be secured? To be spared death, he would have to be taken down from the cross while still alive and come into the care of friends to receive medical attention. Such an alternative presented a problem, but by no means an insoluble one.

We have to let our own imaginations dwell on the requirements as they would have appeared to Jesus. A visit to Golgotha could well have led to the discovery of the tomb in an adjoining plantation. Jesus could have encountered the gardener, who could have provided the information that the property belonged to the rich Jewish councillor Joseph of Arimathaea; or Jesus could have obtained the information in some other way, perhaps from Joseph himself. In any case, it was determined that Joseph's cooperation was essential. He was a man of great influence, with faith in the speedy coming of the Kingdom of God. Because he was devoted to Jesus, he was one who would be ready to carry out meticulously whatever mission might be entrusted to him at great personal risk if the Master required it.

Secretly, in conference with Joseph some four or five months in advance of the events, the plan took shape. For Jesus to escape death, he must appear to have died a very few hours after being crucified. Victims of this form of execution might well remain alive for three days. [See Haim Cohn, *The Trial and Death of Jesus*, (New York: Harper and Row, 1971). Crucifixion was intended to assure a long and lingering death, as Talmudic sources recognized (*Yevamoth xvi and commentaries*).] A drug had to be administered, therefore, which would give the impression of death. This could be provided by the skilled Essenes with their specialized knowledge; their services would be helpful to restore Jesus to health when he regained consciousness. It would be a righteous deed on their part, since they hated the corrupt chief priests and the Roman government as the agents of Satan.

How and when was the drug to be given? Beside the crosses were jars containing a concoction to relieve the anguish of the victims. This could be doctored for Jesus by someone stationed there, when Jesus gave the signal.

We have two principal versions of what happened. Mark, the oldest Gospel, relates that Jesus cried out in Aramaic, "Eloi, Eloi, lama sabachthani?" (My God, my God, why hast thou forsaken me?). Onlookers declared that he was calling for Elijah. One of them then promptly filled a sponge full of "vinegar" and gave him a drink. Almost immediately Jesus "died" (Mark 15:34–37). The presumed eye-witness Gospel, that of John, says that Jesus was given the drink when he had said, "I am thirsty." When he had swallowed the drink, he said, "It is finished," bowed his head, and "died" (John 19:28–30). The accounts agree that the drink was given in response to a cry from Jesus, and that Jesus "expired" almost immediately after receiving it. No Gospel speaks of a drink being given to the two others crucified with Jesus.

Joseph of Arimathaea, possibly with Nicodemus, must have been on hand waiting for the word that the drug had worked, so he could hasten to Pontius Pilate with the request to have the body of Jesus for burial. Pilate was amazed that Jesus had succumbed so quickly and asked the centurion in charge for verification: Pilate then granted Joseph's petition.

Because it was near sunset and the commencement of the Sabbath, those crucified would have had their legs broken to expedite death so their bodies could be taken down and buried before nightfall. Jewish law required that a hanged man's body should not remain overnight unburied, but should be interred the same day (Deuteronomy 21:22–23). On the eve of a Sabbath and festival this provision would especially have demanded respect, even by the Romans, since the instigators of the trial of Jesus had been the chief priests who would have insisted on it. This procedure of breaking the legs of the crucified would have been used on Jesus as well as the two other victims if it had not been for his fortuitous premature demise, a circumstance worthy of note. However, we read in John alone, that the side of Jesus was pierced with a spear, and this unanticipated event would surely have handicapped, if it did not totally destroy, Jesus' chances of recovery.

Nevertheless, what had been prearranged was carried out according to plan. After removing Jesus' body from the cross and taking it to the nearby tomb, herbs and spices were applied to cleanse and staunch the wounds. His body was wrapped in new linen and laid by Joseph and Nicodemus on a horizontal ledge in the cool tomb, there to rest unconscious for the duration of the Sabbath. Thanks to his planning, Jesus could be revived if all went well. He would escape a criminal's burial in a common grave with his fellow sufferers, which would have made restoration impossible.

As soon as practicable after dark on Saturday night, the next task in the plan of operation would be to reopen the tomb, carefully remove the bandages from Jesus, and convey him from the tomb on a litter covered with blankets. Essene doctors would be in attendance to give their expert medical attention as soon as a safe place was reached. After the revival of Jesus, the Essenes would arrange for his convalescence in secret, perhaps at Qumran, and then, as he wished, he would be moved to Galilee where he would be reunited with his disciples. After this, God would disclose His will to His faithful servant.

*   *   *   *

Such a design is indicated by the information and clues available to us. The plan clearly had to be put together with the utmost care and competence, since it gives evidence of thorough observation and research, as well as keen consideration of circumstances and eventualities. The planning was as watertight as human ingenuity could make it, and in many respects it was brilliant, with very little that had not been taken into account. Yet it would appear that something went wrong, which could have had to do with the spear wound inflicted when all seemed to be going so well.

There also might have been a miscalculation in the action of the drug. It is useless to try to identify it. The nature of its ingredients may have been known only to the Essenes, famed for their knowledge of the properties of minerals and plants, and the secret perished with them.

We can only speculate on what happened at the end. Jesus may have been found dead when taken from the tomb, or he

may have died soon afterward, perhaps having regained consciousness briefly. It appears probable that he was moved a considerable distance from the tomb before he actually died or was
found to be dead. The plan seemed to have provided for one of
the Essenes, the young man in white, to remain in the vicinity of
the tomb to give the disciples of Jesus the message that he was
no longer there, having been brought back from the dead, and
that he would be seeing them in Galilee. The man evidently did
not know whether Jesus had succumbed, since he was not
among those transporting Jesus elsewhere.

Those accompanying Jesus would now be in a quandary. His
body could not be taken back to the vacated tomb in broad
daylight. There was only one thing to be done: bury him rever-
ently on the spot. Once faith in the resurrection had taken hold
on the disciples, it was impossible to disclose where Jesus was
interred or how it came about that the tomb near Golgotha was
found open and empty. As for Joseph of Arimathaea, legend has
it that he sailed for Britain, and the Essenes were trained to keep
silence.

But, of course, Jesus did prove to be immortal because of
his worth, and needed neither planning nor miracle to make
him so.

Appendix

In the early days of the Roman Empire under the Julian dynasty and its successor, when the new religion of Christianity was taking shape, the belief was widespread that notable mortals could return from the dead, and even achieve apotheosis, having ascended to heaven. Of the first-century sage, the famous Apollonius of Tyana, it was told that he had manifested himself after death, and some held that he had become a god and did not die. A temple was dedicated to his worship.

The deification of the Roman emperors became well established in the first century A.D., and they were deemed after death on earth to have ascended to heaven as gods. A skit on this belief was written by the philosopher Seneca, a contemporary of the apostle Paul, in his *Apocolocyntosis*. "You demand evidence?" he says. "Right. Ask the man who saw Drusilla *en route* for heaven. He will tell you that he saw Claudius [who was lame] going up too, cloppety-cloppety in his usual fashion. That man just can't help seeing what goes on in the sky." (See J. P. V. D. Balsdon, *The Romans*, pp. 257 ff.)

Very few Christians would seem to be aware, however, of the strong similarity that exists between the image of the death and resurrection of Jesus and that of Romulus, the eponymous founder of Rome. The latter is set down in Plutarch's *Parallel Lives*. Plutarch was born in the reign of the Emperor Claudius (41–54 A.D.) and was a contemporary of the authors of the Gospels. The relevant passage is quoted in full from an old English translation, which gives the flavor of the Authorized Version of the Bible.

Of Romulus, when he vanished, was neither the least part of his body, nor rag of his clothes to be seen; so that some fancied that the Senators having fallen upon him, cut his body into pieces, and each took a part away in his bosom. Others think, his disappearance was neither in the temple of Vulcan, nor with the Senators only present; but that it happened as he was haranguing the people without the city, near a place called the Goats' Marsh; and that on the sudden most wonderful disorders and alterations beyond belief arose in the air; for the face of the sun was darkened, and the day was turned into an unquiet and turbulent night, made up of thunderings and boisterous winds, raising tempests from all quarters, which scattered the rabble and made them fly, but the Senators kept close togther.

The tempest being over, and the light breaking out, when the people gathered again, they missed and enquired for their King; but the Senators would not let them search, or busy themselves about the matter, but commanded them to honour and worship Romulus, as one taken up to the Gods, and who, after having been a good prince, was now to be to them a propitious deity. The multitude hearing this went away rejoicing and worshipping him, in hopes of good things from him.

But there were some who canvassing the matter more severely and rigorously, accused and aspersed the Patricians, as men that persuaded the people to believe ridiculous tales, when they themselves were the murderers of the King. Things being in this disorder, one, they say, of the Patricians, of a noble family, and most approved conversation, and withal a most faithful and familiar friend of Romulus himself, who came with him from Alba, Julius Proculus by name, stepping into the company, and taking an oath by all that was most sacred, protested before them all that Romulus appeared to and met him travelling on the road, comelier and fairer than ever, dressed in shining and flaming armour. And he, being affrighted at the apparition, said, "Upon what occasion or resentments, O King, did you leave us here, liable to most unjust and wicked surmises, and the whole city destitute, in most bitter sorrow?" And that he made answer, "It pleased the Gods, O Proculus, that after we had remained a reasonable time among men, and built a city, the greatest in the world both in empire and glory, we should again return to heaven from whence we came. But be of good heart, and let the Romans know that by the exercise of temperance and fortitude they shall arrive at the highest pitch of human power, and we will be to you the propitious God Quirinus."

This seemed very credible to the Romans, both upon the honesty and oath of him that spoke it; and a certain divine passion, like an enthusiasm, seized on all men, for nobody contradicted it: but laying aside all jealousies and detractions, they prayed to Quirinus, and saluted him God.